F DU

D0437245

POINT LOMA NAZARENE COLLEGE
Ryan Library
3900 Lomaland Drive, San Diego, CA 92106-2899

Call Number   **Accession Number**

150.1952   198873
C239i

Caper, R
IMMATERIAL FACTS

Immaterial Facts

Freud's Discovery of Psychic Reality
and Klein's Development of His Work

150.1952
C239i

Immaterial Facts

*Freud's Discovery of Psychic Reality
and Klein's Development of His Work*

Robert Caper, M.D.

Jason Aronson Inc.
Northvale, New Jersey
London

POINT LOMA NAZARENE COLLEGE
198873
RYAN LIBRARY

Copyright © 1988 by Robert Caper

10 9 8 7 6 5 4 3 2 1

All rights reserved. Printed in the United States of America. No part of this book may be used or reproduced in any manner whatsoever without written permission from *Jason Aronson Inc.* except in the case of brief quotations in reviews for inclusion in a magazine, newspaper, or broadcast.

Library of Congress Cataloging-in-Publication Data

Caper, Robert.
  Immaterial facts.

  Bibliography: p.
  Includes index.
  1. Psychoanalysis.   2. Freud, Sigmund, 1856–1939—
Influence.   3. Klein, Melanie.   I. Title.   [DNLM:
1. Freud, Sigmund, 1856–1939.   2. Klein, Melanie.
3. Psychoanalytic Theory.   WM 460 C239i]
BF173.C35   1988   150.19'5'0922   87–27069
ISBN 0-87668-991-8

Manufactured in the United States of America.

The author gratefully acknowledges permission to reprint portions of the following:

Envy and Gratitude and Other Works 1946–1963, Vol. III by M. Klein, the estate of Melanie Klein and The Hogarth Press, Chatto & Windus Publishers, 1984; The Free Press, a Division of Macmillan, Inc., 1984.

Love, Guilt and Reparation and Other Works 1921–1945, Vol. I by M. Klein, the estate of Melanie Klein and The Hogarth Press, Chatto & Windus Publishers, 1984; The Free Press, a Division of Macmillan, Inc., 1984.

The Standard Edition of the Complete Psychological Works of Sigmund Freud, translated and edited by J. Strachey, Sigmund Freud Copyrights, Ltd., The Institute of Psycho-Analysis, and The Hogarth Press, 1953–1974.

The *Collected Papers of Sigmund Freud,* authorized translation by J. Riviere, A. Strachey, and J. Strachey, Basic Books, Inc., Publishers, by arrangement with The Hogarth Press and The Institute of Psycho-Analysis, London, 1953–1974.

An Autobiographical Study; The Psychopathology of Everyday Life; The Ego and the Id; Group Psychology and the Analysis of the Ego; Inhibitions, Symptoms and Anxiety; New Introductory Lectures on Psychoanalysis; and *Civilization and Its Discontents,* W. W. Norton & Company, Inc., copyright 1933 by Sigmund Freud; © 1935, 1952 by W. W. Norton & Company, Inc.; © 1922, 1959 by The Institute of Psycho-Analysis and Angela Richards; © 1959, 1960, 1961, 1963, 1964, 1965 by James Strachey; © 1959 by Sigmund Freud Copyrights, Ltd.; © 1960 by Alan Tyson; and © 1961 by WJH Sprott.

"Some Thoughts About Tradition and Change Arising from an Examination of the British Psychoanalytical Society's Controversial Discussions (1943–1944)" by R. Steiner, from the *International Review of Psycho-Analysis,* 1985, 12:27–71.

The Brown and the Blue Books by L. Wittgenstein, Basil Blackwell, Ltd., 1958.

The Complete Letters of Sigmund Freud to Wilhelm Fliess, Harvard University Press, 1985.

TO R.L.C.

Contents

Preface and Acknowledgments   *xiii*

Foreword by Hanna Segal   *xv*

Part I. Freud's Discovery of Psychic Reality

Chapter 1.   **Immaterial Facts**   3

        Freud's Early Model of the Mind   8
        Psychic Reality   10
        Psychoanalysis of Children   12

Chapter 2.   **Psychology without a Psyche**   17

        The Seduction Theory   22
        A Scientific Fairy Tale   25

Chapter 3.   **The Discovery of Unconscious Fantasy**   *27*

  Infantile Sexuality   *36*
  The Oedipus Complex   *37*
  The Dynamic Unconscious   *38*

Chapter 4.   **The Structure of Dreams and Neurosis**   *41*

  The Meaning of Dreams   *44*
  Dreams and Neurosis   *48*
  Repression   *49*

Chapter 5.   **Transference and the Crystallization of the Psychoanalytic Method**   *53*

  The Role of Transference in Psychoanalysis   *55*
  The Crystallization of the Psychoanalytic
    Method   *63*
  Free Association   *64*
  Free-Floating Attention   *68*

Chapter 6.   **Gravitational Confinement**   *71*

  The Persistence of Freud's Original Model   *75*
  The Theory of Libido   *76*

Chapter 7.   **A Specimen Case: Little Hans**   *79*

  Case History   *82*
  Freud at the Midpoint of His Development   *89*

Chapter 8.   **Identification and the Structure of the Inner World**   *93*

  Identification   *96*
  The Structure of the Inner World   *99*

Chapter 9.   **Anxiety and the Structure of the Inner World**   *101*

  Abandoning the Libido Theory of Anxiety   *104*
  A Psychological Theory of Anxiety   *105*

Chapter 10. **Beyond Eros** *111*

The Destructive Instinct *114*

Part II. Melanie Klein's Development of Freud's Work

Chapter 11. **Melanie Klein's Place in Psychoanalysis** *121*

Freud's Comments on Klein *126*
Opposition and Acceptance *128*

Chapter 12. **The Method of Child Psychoanalysis** *131*

Klein's Approach to the Psychoanalysis of
   Children *137*
Klein's Technique of Child Analysis *139*
Transference in Children *140*

Chapter 13. **The Child's Construction of Experience** *145*

External Repression *148*
The Child's Internal World *151*

Chapter 14. **Instinct, Fantasy, and Early Psychic
Processes** *157*

Fantasy and Instinct *159*
Unconscious Fantasy and External Reality *161*
Fantasy and Psychological Structure *163*

Chapter 15. **Projective Identification and the Formation of
the Inner World** *167*

The Formation of the Superego *169*
Splitting and the Early Development of the
   Internal Object World *174*
The Paranoid-Schizoid Position *176*
Projective Identification *176*
Projective Identification and the
   Psychoanalysis of Schizophrenia *180*

Chapter 16. **The Transformation of the Superego:**
Psychological Integration and Growth   *183*

    The Depressive Position and the Sense
      of Reality   *191*
    Reparation   *193*
    Manic Defenses and Depressive Illness   *194*
    Reparation, Creativity, and Normal
      Psychological Development   *199*

Chapter 17. **The Early Stages of the Oedipus Complex**   *201*

    Oedipal Development of the Boy   *209*
    Oedipal Development of the Girl   *211*
    The Kleinian Revision of the Oedipus
      Complex   *213*

Chapter 18. **Envy and Gratitude, Splitting and**
Integration   *217*

    Unconscious Envy and Splitting   *223*
    Unconscious Gratitude and Integration   *226*

Chapter 19. **Psychoanalytic Knowledge**   *229*

    Therapeutic Knowledge   *231*
    Theoretical Knowledge   *234*

Chapter 20. **Freud and Klein: A Summary**   *239*

References   *251*

Index   *257*

Preface and Acknowledgments

This book focuses on the relationship between the work of Sigmund Freud, the founder of psychoanalysis, and the work of the British psychoanalyst Melanie Klein, whom many consider to be its second greatest exponent. Klein's work is a development of Freud's in that she built her ideas and her methodology upon his. Her work is, however, a development in another sense: It crystallizes themes that, although fundamentally a part of his thinking, remained latent and undeveloped in Freud's writing. The core of Klein's contribution to psychoanalysis is a detailed and sophisticated unfolding of what is implicit in Freud. Her explication of Freud forms the basis of her many original contributions to psychoanalytic theory.

Psychoanalysis is not a philosophical school with a body of canonical tenets, but, rather, an empirical approach to the mind with its own specific clinical methodology. The congruencies and conflicts between Freud's and Klein's work, therefore, are not by nature philosophical — "Freudian analysis" vs. "Kleinian analysis" —

but are different stages or aspects of a continuous empirical investigation of the mind. Carried out within a definite methodological framework, their work, like all other scientific investigations, proceeds by a series of progressive approximations to the truth.

This book is divided into two parts. The first is an account of how Freud's work evolved from its prepsychoanalytic beginnings into its final form, and the second is a description of the development of Melanie Klein's work from its beginnings, in about 1920, to her death in 1960. The juxtaposition of the work of the two most highly original thinkers in psychoanalysis allows one to form a perspective on psychoanalysis that cannot be gained from the study of either one alone.

Finally, it is a pleasure to be able to acknowledge my debts to Dr. Albert Mason for his support and valuable suggestions during the writing of this book, and in the years that preceded it; to Dr. Donald Rinsley, who has given generous, thoughtful editorial advice; to my friends and colleagues who offered their encouragement; to my patients who have allowed me to use portions of their analyses in the writing of this book; to my family, without whose patience, support and forbearance I could not have written this book; and most of all to my wife, who spent countless hours reading the manuscript and carrying out the monumental task of coaxing me into expressing my thoughts as clearly and succinctly as I could.

Los Angeles

Foreword

There is a lot of confusion, perhaps particularly in the United States, about Melanie Klein's place in the development of psychoanalysis and the relationship between her work and Sigmund Freud's. Occasionally one hears Melanie Klein referred to in the same breath with Jung or Adler—as an opponent of Freudian analysis. Robert Caper's work is, therefore, timely and important because it helps to solidify Klein's position alongside Freud; her work is deeply rooted in Freudian thought. She considered herself to be a developer of Freud's work, building upon his technique and enlarging his ideas by further research, while always remaining faithful to the spirit of his ideas.

Dr. Caper traces the development of Freud's thought, leading from his early model based on a parallel with biology, chemistry, and the physical sciences, to increasingly psychological considerations and the importance of the inner world and its psychic realities. Freud originally thought of anxiety as being caused by repression — the libido is blocked by repression and is converted into anxiety "like wine into vinegar." His discovery that in fact anxiety caused repression led him to explore the sources of anxiety, and he delved even deeper into the realms of the psyche in pursuit of an understanding of psychic conflict. Hence, his early theories of mechanical blockages were increasingly replaced by the notion of central psychological conflict. In 1920, for instance, his theory of the life and death instinct, which he originally thought to be a conflict between sexuality and self-preservation and reality, took him much deeper into the internal sources of conflict. By 1923, in *The Ego and the Id,* he set forth his discovery of the superego, describing it as possessing an internal structure and an internal object.

In *Civilization and Its Discontents*[1] he writes:

> Experience shows however that the severity of the super-ego which a child develops in no way corresponds to the severity of treatment which he himself has met with. The severity of the former seems to be independent of that of the latter (as has rightly been emphasized by Melanie Klein and by other English writers). [p. 130]

With the increased recognition of an internal conflict, Freud gradually gave more recognition to the role played by aggression in both anxiety and guilt.

The development of Melanie Klein, who started working in the 1920s, evolves predominantly from the work of Freud in his later years. Joan Riviere made the following observation in her introduction to *New Developments in Psychoanalysis,* which contains the papers presented by Klein and her co-workers in the "Controversial Discussions" at the British Psycho-Analytical Society:

> Now it is just in this very matter of Freud's own inconsistencies and modifications or later developments in his views — whatever they are to be called — that one of the most conspicuous differences between Melanie Klein and her opponents manifests itself. It becomes clear that those analysts who dispute Melanie Klein's findings most vehemently themselves still stand in the main by

---

[1] *Standard Edition,* vol. 21.

Freud's original formulations which were never fully retraced or abandoned; and that where Freud later broke new ground and went ahead sometimes in more intuitive recognition, they have never followed. [p. 8]

Klein started her analytical work by evolving a technique of psychoanalyzing children, and this illustrates how different she was from other pioneers of her day such as Hug–Helmuth and Anna Freud. She insisted on keeping intact Freud's psychoanalytic posture and technique in psychoanalytic work with children. Realizing that children's natural mode of self-expression is play, she provided them with little toys and interpreted both their verbal communications and their physical actions. She contended that children develop a transference provided one gives them a psychoanalytic setting for expression. This was in contrast to Anna Freud, who believed that children don't develop a transference because "the first edition is not out of print." Klein also believed that children who come to analysis already have a history that is repeated in the transference, and in particular, internal figures in their inner world are projected onto the analyst and form the basis of the transference. In retrospect one can see how comparatively bold this notion was.

Rooted in Melanie Klein's visionary and bold ideas was her complete conviction that the psychoanalytic method was applicable to children as well as adults. Her firsthand work with children, particularly small children, confirmed Freud's preliminary findings on the nature of child development, based on reconstructions of his analysis of adults. Not surprisingly, Klein's direct work with children led her to new discoveries as well. She mapped out the growth of the mental capacities of the brain from infancy onwards, and by illuminating their earlier history and roots, she helped in the understanding of the Oedipus complex and the superego. These insights influenced her work with adults and enabled her to understand and reach more primitive layers of the mind than had been possible before.

Hanna Segal
London

When I had pulled myself together, I was able to draw the right conclusions from my discovery: namely that neurotic symptoms were not related directly to actual events but to wishful phantasies, and that as far as the neurosis was concerned, psychical reality was of more importance than material reality.

— Sigmund Freud, *An Autobiographical Study*

From its inception analysis has always laid stress on the importance of the child's earliest experiences, but it seems to me that only since we know more about the nature and contents of its early anxieties, and about the continuous interplay between its actual experiences and its phantasy-life, can we fully understand why *the external factor is so important.*

— Melanie Klein, "A Contribution to the Psychogenesis of Manic-Depressive States"

Immaterial Facts

*Freud's Discovery of Psychic Reality
and Klein's Development of His Work*

PART I

Freud's Discovery of
Psychic Reality

1

Immaterial Facts

*D*o we have a feeling of familiarity whenever we look at familiar objects? Or do we have it usually? When do we actually have it? It helps us to ask: what do we contrast the feeling of familiarity with? One thing we contrast it with is surprise. One could say: "Unfamiliarity is much more of an experience than familiarity."

— Ludwig Wittgenstein

In 1833, a Canadian voyageur named Alexis St. Martin suffered an accidental gunshot wound that never healed, leaving him with a permanent hole in the left side of his abdomen leading into his stomach. Dr. William Beaumont, the United States Army surgeon who treated him, arranged to keep St. Martin in his employ for several years in order to fully utilize this splendid opportunity for observing gastric physiology directly. His observations are consid-

ered to be of great value even today. In the straight-faced language
of medicine, such events are known as "experiments of nature."

Over the years, such experiments have provided physicians and
physiologists with important, and otherwise unobtainable, insights
into human physiology. In other species, such knowledge may be
gained in the laboratory. For example, it is relatively easy to
discover what part a dog's pancreas plays in its well being: One
simply removes it, observes that the animal develops diabetes, and
concludes that the pancreas had some role in preventing the disease.
It is at best difficult, however, to be certain if the same is true in
humans. One must wait for someone to lose his pancreas to
inflammation, cancer, or, perhaps, a gunshot. Our knowledge of
those human functions not paralleled in other species depends
entirely on these "experiments."

In his book *Learning from Experience* (1962), the psychoanalyst
Wilfred Bion describes a psychological equivalent of St. Martin's
gunshot wound. He writes of a patient whose thought processes
lacked the qualities of depth, resonance, and evocativeness that one
associates with the human mind, and so seemed to be the product
not of a mind, but of a machine. From the data of the patient's
analysis, Bion draws a picture of the mental organ whose impair-
ment resulted in this state of affairs and reconstructs circumstances
that might have led to it. This reconstruction is worth recounting in
some detail.

Bion begins by taking seriously the commonplace notion that,
just as infants need physical care and comfort, they must also
receive love.[1] From this it follows that an infant must have the
capacity to perceive love — have a sense organ for love — much as it has
sense organs for perceiving food and warmth.

He considers what might happen if something interfered with
the infant's ability to absorb those of its mother's states of mind that
constitute its emotional sustenance. This could occur if, for exam-

---

[1]This idea has been driven home by Schlossman's classic observations of
hospitalism (1926): There is a dramatic and unaccountably high mortality rate
among unwanted infants housed in large orphanage wards whose physical needs
were tended to with great efficiency by a staff too busy to make emotional contact
with them.

ple, the infant were unable to bear the emotional strain of realizing that its well-being—and even its survival—depends on something as intangible as its mother's love. In its horror of needing what is intangible, and therefore not possessable, the infant blinds itself to its need for love, solace, and understanding. Starved of the requirements for mental and emotional growth, but unable to grasp them, it redoubles its desperate efforts to obtain what it can still perceive: material satisfactions divorced from emotional gratification.

In consequence, the infant grows into an adult like Bion's machinelike patient, who greedily pursued every form of material comfort in a vain effort to supply himself with the nonmaterial comfort he lacked but could not recognize. He eventually comes to live in a perceptual world composed only of material objects, and since one can identify only with what one can perceive, he inevitably becomes like a material object himself, a state of affairs reflected in his machine-like thought processes. To Bion, this represents a "breakdown in the patient's equipment for thinking" about emotional realities, which leaves him living in a universe populated by emotionless objects that Bion calls "inanimate."

Bion then moves beyond the immediate clinical problem to reflect on one of greater significance:

> The scientist whose investigations include the stuff of life itself finds himself in a situation that has a parallel in that of the patients I am describing. . . . It appears that our rudimentary equipment for "thinking" thoughts is adequate when the problems are associated with the inanimate, but not when the object for investigation is the phenomena of life itself. . . . [This] means that the field for investigation, all investigation being ultimately scientific, is limited, by human inadequacy, to those phenomena which have the characteristics of the inanimate. We assume that the psychotic limitation is due to an illness: but that of the scientist is not. Investigation of this assumption illuminates disease on one hand and scientific method on the other. . . . Confronted with the complexities of the human mind the analyst must be circumspect in following even accepted scientific method; its weakness may be closer to the weakness of psychotic thinking than superficial scrutiny would admit. [1962, p. 14]

The problem Bion has formulated is this: The scientific methods and modes of thought that are appropriate to an understanding of the inanimate world (such as those of physics or chemistry), or to an understanding of the mechanical aspects of biological or social systems (such as those of physiology and behaviorism), yield models that are mechanical and therefore inappropriate for understanding states of mind. How, then, may we arrive at a description of the mind without falling prey to the scientific version of what crippled Bion's patient—an inability to think about emotional realities that restricts (perhaps disastrously) our thoughts and imagination to the realm of the inanimate?

Freud's Early Model of the Mind

The pitfall implied in this question awaits anyone who ventures to construct a scientific model of the mind. It snared even Freud, whose original, prepsychoanalytic model of the mind was a mechanical one of precisely the type Bion warns us against. Freud's development as a psychoanalyst may be viewed as a progressive and generally successful attempt to extricate himself from it.

Freud's early model portrayed the mind simply as a network of neurons in which electrical charges were stored and transmitted. These charges arose under the physical impact of environmental stimuli—light, sound waves, the pressure of physical contact on the skin, and so on. The overriding principles that governed the apparatus were the physical laws of thermodynamics, which dictated that its internal energy level must always be kept as low as possible. This meant that the mind needed to discharge continuously the energy it acquired from environmental stimuli. Hysteria, which this model was devised to explain, was the result of the system's failure to discharge energy in the normal, thermodynamic manner. The build-up of excess energy could be relieved, however, if the stimulus that gave rise to it in the first place (and that had been forgotten) could be recalled in a vivid fashion.

Freud believed that the forgotten, offending stimulus was a sexual trauma that the patient had been subjected to in childhood. The therapist's job was to expose this memory by tracking it down through a chain of associated thoughts, starting with the patient's account of his or her symptoms and working back through time to the buried memory. Freud believed that the ideas whose path he was following were connected only by virtue of their being impressions of events that had occurred close to one another in time or space. Tracing a hysterical symptom to its source therefore meant following a chain of associations whose connections were accidents of space and time, and therefore meaningless.

Freud's model illustrates our tendency to picture our minds as some familiar type of technological apparatus. The great British neurologist Sherrington, for example, compared the mind to a telegraphic network; Leibniz likened it to a mill; and the Greeks, it is said, spoke of the mind as a kind of catapult. In Freud's model the mind worked like a series of electrical capacitors.

Bion's patient, insofar as he was unable to perceive or appreciate the emotional realities of himself or his world, had a mind that would be adequately modeled by such a mechanical system. The severity of his disorder is a measure of the limitations of a mechanical model of the mind.

Now, as Freud set about trying to confirm his neurological model of hysteria by retrieving from his patients the memories of the external events that he supposed had triggered the electrical derangement in the apparatus, he was confounded by the intrusion into their associations of something other than the memories he was looking for. Some of what his patients told him was undoubtedly derived from half-forgotten experiences, but their accounts of their past also contained elements derived from fantasies. Although these fantasies were themselves unconscious, they produced in the patient's conscious mind spurious "memories" that were, as far as the patient was concerned, indistinguishable from dim memories of actual childhood events. Freud realized that he could not himself reliably distinguish in patients' stories what was history from what was history colored by fantasy, or even what was pure fantasy. The intrusion of unconscious fantasy cast a cloud over his whole project.

Because Freud could not eliminate this influence on his search for the source of hysteria, he began to study it. He saw that his patients were unable to distinguish these fantasies from memories of actual events not because they were psychotic—which they weren't—but because of a peculiarity of the fantasies concerned. The fantasies were all unconscious, laden with emotion, and usually contained some kernel of truth, however minuscule and distorted. They portrayed events as the patient might, for one reason or another, have desired them to be. The unconscious, in other words, contains, in addition to faithful memories of material events, fantasies that are amalgams of memory and desire, and the two kinds of idea have precisely the same effect on the mind. The methodologic obstacle that this presented to Freud's neurological model, which rested on the accurate retrieval of unconscious memories of actual events, was insuperable.

Psychic Reality

But then, over a period of months, Freud realized that this disastrous turn of events really didn't matter after all, because his notion that material events made a direct impact on the mind was quite irrelevant to the study of neurosis. What mattered in the unconscious, at least as far as neurotic symptoms were concerned, was not the memory of external events, but how the patient had experienced them. It was, in other words, the subjective meaning of events, not their physiologic impact on the mental apparatus, that counted.

But the unconscious, subjective meaning of events is precisely what was represented in his patients' unconscious fantasies about their history. The obstacle to Freud's pursuit of a neurological solution was the key to a new kind of solution based on the subjective meaning of experience. What he needed to concern himself with were not buried memories per se, but the mixture of perception and emotion-laden fantasy that was the unconscious version of memory. He named this mixture *psychic reality*. In neurosis, he said, psychic reality is of greater importance than material reality.

This realization opened the way to a new kind of model of the mind, built on the investigation of psychic reality, that could avoid the pitfalls of the old mechanical models. In psychic reality, experiences and ideas are infused with meaning by the subject's fears and desires. The concept of psychic reality entails emotional significance, the necessity of which was made so dramatically obvious by its absence in Bion's patient. This is what made the new model revolutionary. By shifting his attention away from raw historical events and toward the melding of external reality with instinct-driven wishes and fears, Freud became a psychoanalyst.

To delineate and trace the unconscious emotional significance that events had for his patients, Freud needed to develop in himself a capacity to attend to the emotionality concealed in their words. This capacity is the ability to focus on patterns of psychological phenomena that seem at first to be meaningless or obscure, but that become inescapably meaningful when carefully observed. He needed, that is, to become a phenomenologist of unconscious meanings. Freud (1893) records how impressed he was when he first encountered a careful phenomenologist at work in the person of his teacher, the great French neurologist Charcot, who

> used to look again and again at things he did not understand, to deepen his impression of them day by day, till suddenly an understanding of them dawned on him. In his mind's eye the apparent chaos presented by the continual repetition of the same symptoms then gave way to order. . . . He remarked again and again on the difficulty and the value of this kind of "seeing." He would ask why it was that in medicine people only see what they have already learned to see. [p. 12]

Charcot was able to see what he had previously overlooked for so long by remaining in contact with doubts and mysteries — the unexplained details presented by clinical phenomena — without embarking, in Keats's words, on "an irritable search after fact and reason." When Freud's attempt to verify his neurological theory of hysteria ran afoul of his patients' unconscious fantasies, he recalled his experience with Charcot, and he began to observe his patients' states of mind as carefully as his teacher had the disordered movements of their bodies. His respect for the phenomenologic details of his patients' emotional realities, regardless of how little sense they made at first, allowed him eventually to recognize their patterns and thus their crucial importance in the life of the mind.

Unlike sciences that are based on the perception of material facts, psychoanalysis is based on the perception of immaterial facts: psychological states in oneself and others. Freud called the faculty that enables us to perceive these "the organ for the perception of psychical qualities." The systematic use of this organ — the one that a "natural experiment" had destroyed in Bion's patient — constitutes the psychoanalytic method, out of which emerges all the evidence on which psychoanalytic theories rest.

Armed with this clinical methodology, Freud explored and roughly mapped out vast reaches of the unconscious, a process he later compared to the exploits of the conquistadors. His phenomenologic investigation of psychic reality, the locus of unconscious emotional meaning, produced a new model of the mind whose elements were meaning and emotion. This model, his most fundamental innovation, permitted him to arrive at an understanding first of dreams and then of neurosis, and finally at a rational method of treatment of neurosis.

Freud did not, however, abandon his neurological viewpoint entirely when he adopted the psychoanaltyic one. His subsequent work was a mixture of the new psychoanalytic model and the older neurological model, elements of which he retained like cherished relics. The work of many of his successors has been a similar mixture of psychoanalytic and mechanical perspectives on the mind.

Psychoanalysis of Children

The British psychoanalyst Melanie Klein is an outstanding exception. The most striking feature of her work is the purity of its psychoanalytic perspective: her single-minded dedication to the phenomenology of emotional meaning. She was the first to devise a means of systematically investigating the unconscious psychic reality of children, a technical development that opened the way to the psychoanalysis of children. Her work with children showed that Freud's concept of psychic reality — and therefore psychoanalysis — had descriptive and explanatory power that exceeded even that realized by Freud himself.

This may be seen, for example, in the question of the nature of the infant's mind—or rather, of whether infants have minds. To the end of his life, Freud believed that the infant's mind would turn out to be the kind of electrophysiologic apparatus, free of the complexities of emotional meaning, that he had originally hoped to find in the adult neurotic. His freedom to hold this view was enhanced by an almost complete absence of psychoanalytic data on the subject.

As Klein's analyses of children began to supply the missing data, she was led inevitably to the conclusion that the minds of even small children and infants were far too complex, and turned too much on psychologically meaningful fantasies, to be fitted into a framework devoid of emotional significance. That is, she found that the complex logic of psychic reality not only could be but had to be employed to make sense of even the comparatively "simple" mind of the small child and infant. Although this complexity seemed improbable, it was perhaps no more improbable than Freud's discovery that certain unconscious fantasies were functionally equivalent to memories. In any event, it was what her contact with the child's unconscious indicated, and she tailored her theories to follow the implications of her phenomenologic findings.

Among the unconscious fantasies that shape children's experience of their world, Klein found one group in particular that was crucial to her views on the developments of the child's mind. Children and infants have a fantasy that they create a world within themselves by "swallowing" parts of the external world. This internal world is not an accurate image of the external one, but is colored when the child (also in fantasy) injects his or her own emotions into the external world during the process of swallowing it. Klein called this process "the balanced interplay of projection and introjection." It is the instrument that builds what Freud recognized as psychic reality, producing a fantastic world that infants experience as concrete, actually situated inside themselves, and populated by versions of those they love and hate. This inner world is no metaphor for the child, who experiences it as his or her real psychological inside, or what we from an adult perspective would call the mind. The nature of this inner world and its populace fluctuates according to the child's state of mind, or rather, constitutes those states of mind. Klein called the elements of which this inner world is composed "internal objects."

The child's relationship to these internal objects could be classified into two major modes, or "positions," distinguishable from each other by their characteristic constellations of unconscious fantasies, anxieties, and defenses. The earlier of the two, the paranoid-schizoid position (so-called because failure to negotiate it successfully in the course of development rendered one prone in later life to paranoid and schizophrenic illnesses), was gradually superseded by the later one, the depressive position (so-named because failure to work through its conflicts and anxieties during development produced a vulnerability to later depressive illness).

Although it is hardly surprising that Freud's work provides an introduction to Klein's—his work does, after all, provide the foundation for the work of every other psychoanalyst—what is surprising is the degree to which Klein's work serves as a kind of introduction to Freud's. Because Klein observed the unfolding of the child's psychic reality at an earlier stage of development than had Freud, the central findings from his analyses of adults are themselves developmental consequences of what Klein found in her analyses of children. Had her work on infancy and the unconscious of children come first, much of his work on the unconscious of adults would have fulfilled the predictions that one would have made on the basis of hers.

An example of this is Freud's theory of the Oedipus complex, the central element in his picture of emotional development. He found that the child undergoes a crisis when the Oedipus complex reaches its peak at age 4 or 5, the resolution of which has profound implications for the psychological health of the adult. Klein's work showed that the Freudian Oedipus complex has such great psychological moment because it is a watershed for the child's struggles to resolve the even earlier developmental conflicts, themselves rooted in infancy, of the paranoid-schizoid and depressive positions. The Oedipus complex is a major vehicle through which the child accomplishes this, and its various themes are the result of the child's efforts to harmonize the parts of the inner and outer worlds so that psychological development may proceed.

Even more striking than Klein's findings being a developmental prologue to Freud's is the fact that the areas of his work that would not seem to follow from Klein's—his theory of female sexuality, the

libido theory, and his dating of superego formation, for example —
also have not withstood the test of time and have fallen out of what
is considered useful analytic theory, even in the opinion of psychoanalysts who do not subscribe to Klein's findings.

But of course Klein's work historically could not have preceded
Freud's. His development and testing of psychoanalytic methodology on the (relatively!) firm ground of the adult psychoanalytic
consulting room was a scientific prerequisite for her fathoming the
child's unconscious, so much further removed from ordinary adult
conscious experience. Only with the accumulation of clinical experience, and the consequent development of analytic theories and
methods to the point where they became sturdy enough to guide the
investigation of the more primitive levels of the mind, could the
psychoanalytic picture of the mind's growth (and the internal logic of
psychoanalytic theory) be extended beyond Freud's work. The
chapters that follow will outline both the Freudian and the Kleinian
phases of this broader development and the mutually illuminating
relationship between the work of its two main architects.

2

Psychology without a Psyche

F reud began his medical career as a neurologist, and his first approach to the study of psychological disturbance resulted in an unpublished, speculative neurophysiological treatise that appeared only posthumously under the title of "Project for a Scientific Psychology" (1950). His own title for it, more to the point, was "Psychology for Neurologists." It is couched in terms of the distribution and flow of charges and energy, a way of thinking that dovetailed with the program for the development of science espoused by the influential physicist and physiologist Helmholtz. The treatise's motto might even have been the proclamation made by Helmholtz 25 years before Freud wrote it: "The ultimate objective of the natural sciences is to reduce all processes in nature to the movements that underlie them and to find their driving forces, that is, to reduce them to mechanics." (Mayr 1982, p. 115).

In reading the "Project," one gets the impression not of a psychology in its own right but rather of a new branch of physiology, whose expositor is a bit embarrassed about not providing the reader with the kind of precision one would find in a physicist's treatise on the motion of fluids. Because it is an attempt to describe the phenomena that underlie mental life in terms of electrical forces, psychological states appear in the "Project" only as symptoms of physical processes, like the whistle of a steam engine.

Freud wrote two other works at the same time, a book written in collaboration with his friend and senior colleague, Josef Breuer, titled *Studies on Hysteria* (1895), and a paper on "The Neuro-Psychoses of Defence" (1894). These two works, together with the "Project," show how Freud's thinking was dominated during the mid-1890s by attempts to construct a psychology without a psyche.

As the editor and translator of Freud's complete works in English, James Strachey pointed out that the model of the mind Freud presented in the "Project" rested on the recent discovery that the microscopic structure of the nervous system consisted of discrete, threadlike branching cells called neurons, which lie in physical contact with each other to form a network. Freud assumed that these neurons could become excited by being filled with some form of physical energy capable of being transferred from one neuron to another throughout the network.

This model provided an explanation on conservative physiologic lines for a clinical phenomenon in which Freud had become quite interested in the early 1890s. His collaborative work with Breuer in treating patients suffering from hysteria had shown that, under the pressure of the physician's insistence, a patient could trace each symptom[1] back through a chain of intermediate ideas and memories to the event that immediately preceded their first appearance. If the patient could be gotten to recall this event with sufficient clarity and emotional vividness, the symptoms—which had proven intractable to all other forms of therapy—would disappear, at least for the time being. Breuer and Freud called this method of treatment *catharsis*.

In the "chain of associations" back through which he led his

---

[1]The symptoms of hysteria consisted of paralyses, tics, fainting, convulsions, muteness, and amnesias for which no physical cause had been identified.

patients to the precipitating event, Freud saw the interconnections and branching pathways of the network of neurons. From this it was a small step to picture the ideas, memories, and emotions themselves as the actual quantities of energy postulated in his model to occupy cerebral neurons.

Furthermore, the emotional catharsis involved in the recollection of the trauma suggested to Freud a discharge of the stored-up neuronal energy that supposedly filled the group of neurons corresponding to the symptom, rendering them physically inactive, and thus erasing the symptom. From this point of view, the emotions and ideas connected with symptoms had the same significance as the deflection of a needle on a physicist's gauge, indicating the presence of an electrical field. As a medical scientist, Freud's real concern would be with the energies which underlay states of mind, but not with these states per se.

In the concluding section of "The Neuro-Psychoses of Defence" Freud summarizes his picture in the following way:

> I should like, finally, to dwell for a moment on the working hypothesis which I have made use of in this exposition of the neuroses of defence. I refer to the concept that in mental functions something is to be distinguished—a quota of affect or sum of excitation—which possesses all the characteristics of a quantity (though we have no means of measuring it), which is capable of increase, diminution, displacement and discharge, and which is spread over the memory-traces of ideas somewhat as an electric charge is spread over the surface of a body.
>
> This hypothesis, which, incidentally, already underlies our theory of "abreaction" [the relief of psychological symptoms by means of a cathartic emotional experience] . . . can be applied in the same sense as the physicists apply the hypothesis of a flow of electric fluid. It is provisionally justified by its utility in co-ordinating and explaining a great variety of psychical states. [1894, p. 61]

"Throughout this period," Strachey says, "Freud appears to have regarded these . . . processes as *material* events" (1962, p. 64). Having found a physical explanation of what hysterical symptoms were and how to remove them, Freud needed only a congruent explanation of how they arose in the first place to complete his theory of hysteria as a neurophysiological disorder.

The Seduction Theory

If one considers the symptoms of hysteria to arise from a mass of undischarged energy in the neuronal network, as Freud did, the question of the cause of hysteria becomes the question of why this energy remained in the system over a period of months or years instead of being discharged at once.[2] Freud addressed this problem by assuming that the hysteric's mental apparatus violated ordinary thermodynamic behavior because it had somehow been physically damaged.

To support this notion he draws a parallel between hysteria and another neurotic disorder, anxiety neurosis. He was at the time greatly influenced by the theories of his friend and colleague Wilhelm Fliess, who believed that disturbances in sexual physiology lay at the root of a great many illnesses whose appearance would not at first suggest it. Freud had regularly obtained from his anxiety neurotics a history of sexual frustration, and he had constructed a model of the illness along the following lines:

> [Normally] physical sexual excitation above a certain value arouses psychical libido, which then leads to coitus, and so on. If the specific reaction [orgasm] fails to occur, the physicopsychic tension (the sexual affect) increases immeasurably. It becomes disturbing, but there is still no ground for its transformation [into anxiety]. In anxiety neurosis, however, such a transformation does occur, and this suggests the idea that things go wrong in the following way. The physical tension increases, reaches the threshold value at which it can arouse psychic affect; but for

---

[2]The assumption that the neural apparatus would ordinarily tend to discharge whatever energy it contained was based on the idea that the system would obey the principles of thermodynamics, a branch of physics developed to describe the behavior of steam engines and similar systems. Freud's approaching this question so seriously indicated how unquestioningly physical his concept of the mind was at that time.

> several reasons the psychical linkage offered to it remains
> insufficient: a *sexual affect* cannot be formed, because there is
> something lacking in the psychic determinants. Accordingly, the
> physical tension, not being psychically bound, is transformed
> into—anxiety. [Freud 1985, pp. 80–81]

In other words, if sexual excitation fails to reach consciousness
where it may be adequately worked over (discharged), it backs up
into a pool of excitations in the brain, where it manifests itself as
anxiety.

Now, the failure of sexual excitation to reach consciousness (or
as Freud put it, the insufficiency of the psychical linkage offered to
it) was itself the result of a traumatic derangement of the apparatus.
The trauma consisted of the repeated buildup of sexual excitation
that had followed the normal pathway into consciousness, but which
could not be discharged *for external reasons*. In other words, anxiety
neurosis was the result of enforced sexual abstinence. The effect of
all this was to produce a congestion of undischarged sexual excitations, which damaged the part of the brain responsible for pro-
cessing sexual impulses, presumably by overloading it. Later impulses could not traverse the damaged part of the pathway, and
therefore got deflected into the lower regions of the brain where they
were experienced not as sexual excitation but anxiety.

The link between hysteria and anxiety neurosis from the
physical point of view was the production of a large amount of
neuronal excitation that could not be discharged. Freud believed
that the cluster of excitations active in hysteria was, as in anxiety
neurosis, sexual in nature.[3]

If his assumptions about the sexual origins of anxiety in anxiety
neurosis were true, and if his extrapolation to hysteria was valid,
then in hysteria as well there must be some damage in the part of the
apparatus concerned with sexual stimuli. This explanation raised
another problem, however: In anxiety neurosis, the system could

---

[3]When asked several years after he made this formulation why he postulated only
sexual impulses as the source of trouble, Freud replied that he saw no reason in
principle why other impulses could not also be implicated, but his analyses of
patients had turned up only sexual ones. As we shall see, his analyses began later
on to turn up other kinds of elemental unconscious impulses.

not discharge because it had been damaged by the traumatic effects of masses of sexual excitations whose accumulation was due to external, social factors. But in hysteria there was no history of traumatic sexual excitation. Freud answered this difficulty by postulating that the predisposing cause of hysteria—that is, the cause of the damage to the mental apparatus—had nonetheless been an actual unmanageable sexual experience, although in this case one that could not be remembered and would therefore not appear in a history given by the patient. Now he had the specific etiology he was looking for: A hysteric was someone who had been *predisposed* by a traumatic sexual excitation to react to normal sexual excitation in an abnormal way—by developing the symptoms of hysteria. The predisposing excitation was overwhelming because it could not be discharged at the time it occurred. But this left the problem of why, if the patient had experienced such a trauma, there was no history of it.

Freud's answer was that in the case of hysteria, the sexual excitation occurred prior to puberty, when the sexual apparatus was immature and incapable of discharging the excitation through orgasm. The inability of the apparatus to discharge the excitation was what made it traumatic. Freud believed that a trauma occurring in childhood would produce a wider disruption of the whole apparatus than one occurring in adulthood, as in anxiety neurosis. This explained the loss of memory for the event. The specific cause was then a sexual molestation, "an irritation of the genitals," occurring, he thought, somewhere between the ages of 2 or 3 and 7 years. This was the trauma (or seduction) theory of hysteria.

Freud's seduction theory of symptom formation in hysteria appealed to him not because he thought there was any value in seeing his patients as victims, but because it was entirely in line with his picture of the mind as a physical apparatus. He was attracted to it because the operative level of events was that of "forces equal in dignity to the chemical–physical forces inherent in matter."

His now complete model of hysteria was as follows: Physical energy was deposited into the neural apparatus of a vulnerable and passive child by means of an "irritation of the genitals." It could not be discharged due to the child's incapacity for orgasm. The deposition of undischarged energy had a traumatic (damaging) effect on the neural apparatus, in consequence of which later sexual excitations could not discharge themselves normally, but remained instead to accumulate in the apparatus as a reservoir of energy literally powering the tics, convulsions, and other manifestations of hysteria.

This model also suggested a method of curing hysteria. If the memory of the traumatic event was an isolated cluster of excitations that acted like an electrical abscess exerting pressure on the mental apparatus to prevent the normal discharge of incoming stimuli, and thereby predisposed the patient to the production of hysterical symptoms, he could cure the disease by lancing the abscess. Up to this point, he had been successful only in alleviating the *manifest* symptoms of hysteria by the use of Breuer's cathartic technique, but not the predisposition itself. If he could penetrate through to the original cluster of traumatic excitations responsible for the derangement of the neural discharge pathways, he would have cured hysteria permanently. Accordingly, he began to go after the original trauma with considerable therapeutic enthusiasm. By capitalizing on his authority as a physician, he prevailed upon his patients to associate along the lines his theory had laid out for them. He reported with satisfaction in 1895 that his search for the repressed memories of the original trauma had been successful in each of the 18 cases he had treated up to that time.

A Scientific Fairy Tale

Freud believed that he was well on the road to a scientific understanding of neurosis that not only fell handily under the aegis of physical science, but also suggested a rational, effective treatment. After formulating this model of the causes and cure of hysteria, he presented it to his colleagues in the Vienna Medical Society. But his hopes were dashed by Richard von Krafft-Ebing, the president of the society, who expressed the prevailing reaction to Freud's presentation when he pronounced it a "scientific fairy tale." Their condemnation of his work did not mean that they thought he was on the wrong track in seeking the physical basis of hysteria, but merely that his theories, while plausible, had outrun the evidence sup-

198873

porting them. But this assessment stung Freud deeply, and he never quite forgave them for it.

As it happened, Freud eventually did abandon his physical model of hysteria, not because of its rejection by the Viennese medical establishment but because, as he began to look at his patients less with the zealous gaze of the scientific programmatist, and more with the cool gaze of Charcot, he noticed details in their mental lives that had previously escaped his attention. Seeing the patterns into which these details fell produced a shift in his perspective profound enough to make the question of the physical basis of hysteria largely irrelevant.

3

The Discovery of Unconscious Fantasy

In September 1897, after devoting years to the creation of the physical model of hysteria he had considered so promising, Freud suddenly made the dramatic private confession in a letter (Freud 1985) to his friend Wilhelm Fliess that he no longer believed in it. He gave four reasons for his change of heart.

First, he had found that his technique of guiding the patient's associations toward the repressed memory of sexual molestation — which he had adopted on the basis of his belief that such a repressed memory was a kind of psychological abscess, and which he hoped would produce a cathartic emotional release leading to the permanent cure of hysteria — had met with a uniform lack of therapeutic success. This meant that the successes he had claimed for the 18 cases reported on a few years before were in reality "only partial," as he now delicately put it, and that these partial successes could be explained in ways simpler and more conventional than the seduction hypothesis.

Second, to verify his model of hysteria, he needed to demonstrate an actual memory of the sexual molestation that had predisposed the patient to the illness. In no case had he succeeded in meeting this scientific goal. He had apparently relied on conscious (not even, as his theory demanded, repressed) memories in a few cases and on hints that seemed to indicate a repressed memory in the rest. But the existence of such a repressed memory was never confirmed by a vivid recollection. Although he still believed in the reality of seduction in principle, his lack of success in this made him wonder if the confirmation he had sought was not unobtainable in practice. His hope of recovering such a memory was also dampened by the observation that even "in the most deep-reaching psychosis the unconscious memory does not break through, so that the secret of childhood [sexual] experiences is not betrayed even in the most confused delirium" (Freud 1985, p. 265).

Third, the theory demanded that childhood sexual molestation be even more prevalent than hysteria, itself already rather highly prevalent. Most of the data he had gathered from his patients pointed to the father as the guilty party. This meant that if his patients' associations pointed to an actual event in childhood, the incidence of child molestation among bourgeois Jewish Viennese fathers was nearly universal. He considered this unlikely.

Fourth, he had realized that in the unconscious there is "no indication of reality." This meant that certain unconscious fantasies cannot be distinguished from memories of real events, which made identification of a genuine memory extremely problematic. His cathartic method of directing the patient to the pathogenic event gave him no way of knowing whether he was tracking an unconscious memory or an unconscious fantasy.

This last problem was the most formidable, and in the end his search for the specific physiological etiology of hysteria, the repressed memory of a traumatic sexual event, went aground on the shoals of unconscious fantasy. But this was a most salubrious misfortune, for it forced him to go back and listen to his patients not with a theoretician's ear but with a phenomenologist's. As his attention to unconscious fantasy grew, his perspective on the whole problem of hysteria gradually reversed itself until, in the end, he developed a new model based not on physical processes but on states of mind, especially those dominated by the unconscious fantasies that had been such an.obstacle for him before. Where his physical model had welded environmental influences directly to neural processes, excluding psychology, the new model was centered precisely on what had been absent from the old one; it was a genuine psychology. In the steady correspondence Freud maintained with Fliess, we have a record through which this development can be traced.

Freud's first glimmering of the role of unconscious fantasy in hysteria appears in a letter of April 1897, when he wrote that his efforts at recovering the memory of seduction had revealed "a different source from which a new element of the product of the unconscious arises. What I have in mind are hysterical fantasies . . . " (Freud 1985, p. 234).

By the beginning of May 1897, he felt that he had defined more clearly the role of fantasy in neurosis:

> I have gained a sure inkling of the structure of hysteria. Everything goes back to the reproduction of scenes [of molestation]: some can be obtained directly, others always by way of fantasies set up in front of them. . . . [These fantasies] are protective structures, sublimations of the facts, embellishments of them, and at the same time serve for self-relief. Their accidental origin is perhaps from masturbation fantasies. A second important piece of insight tells me that the psychic structures which, in hysteria, are affected by repression are not in reality memories—since no one indulges in memory activity without a motive—but *impulses* which arise from primal scenes [of molestation]. . . . In this I see a great advance in insight. . . . [Freud 1985, p. 239]

He had discovered that the contents of the unconscious part of the mind, which were kept in place by a process he called repression, included fantasies as well as memories. This letter shows that at first he considered fantasies only as defensive structures interfering with his attempts to detect the true cause of hysteria, the repressed memory of an actual traumatic sexual molestation. But at the same time he had come to the conclusion that it was not simply an unobtainable memory of a sexual molestation that was the pathogenic irritant in hysteria, but rather something having to do with the child's impulses. This consideration began to point him in quite a different direction.

By the end of May he could write that "memories appear to bifurcate: One part of them is put aside and replaced by fantasies; another accessible part seems to lead directly to impulses. Is it possible that, later on, impulses can also derive from fantasies?" (Freud 1985, p. 250). He was now occupied with the web of impulse, fantasy, and memory, which had displaced his original search for a repressed memory of an external event. He was also beginning to wonder if children's sexual impulses could arise directly from their fantasies without having been provoked by physical stimulation at the hands of a molester.

In July he came to the conclusion that repressed fantasies and impulses (and in particular perverse sexual impulses) could be even more important than actual memories in producing hysterical symptoms: "What we are faced with are falsifications of memories and fantasies—these latter relating to the past or future. I know roughly the rules in accordance with which these structures are put together and the reasons why they are stronger than genuine memories, and I have thus learnt new things about the characteristics of the processes in the unconscious" (Freud 1985, p. 255). He also added, as an aside, that the general psychology of neuroses was given "in a nutshell" by dreams.

Finally, in the letter of September 1897 mentioned at the start of this chapter, he realized that he must abandon his trauma theory of hysteria. As we can see from the letters leading up to this one, his attention had been gradually drawn away from the question of traumatic etiology and had gotten absorbed by the connections between memory, impulse, fantasy, and motive that he encountered more or less serendipitously in the course of his attempts to verify it. He was now at least partially aware that his attempt to base psychology on physics had led him into a near-fatal oversimplification. His letters also indicate that, in his zeal to establish his theory, he had accepted evidence of seduction that was, to put it mildly, flimsy.

This may have accounted for the incongruous note with which he ended the September letter to Fliess, in which he acknowledged that his dream of a physical model of hysteria had been shattered:

If I were depressed, confused or exhausted, such doubts would surely have to be interpreted as signs of weakness. Since I am in the opposite state, I must recognize them as the result of honest and vigorous intellectual work and must be proud that after going so deep I am still capable of such criticism. Can it be that this doubt merely represents an episode in advance toward further insight?

It is strange, too, that no feeling of shame appeared—for which, after all, there could well be occasion. Of course I shall not tell it in Dan nor speak of it in Askelon, in the land of the Philistines, but in your eyes and my own, I have more the feeling of victory than of a defeat (which is surely not right). [Freud 1985, p. 265]

The trauma theory had forced him to look for an external agency that would excite the child physically. Now Freud could also consider the effects of fantasies, arising spontaneously within a child, which the child could read into even an innocuous or insignificant event, to produce an experience that was spurious in the historical sense but real in a psychological one—he could, in other words, now encompass within his model the idiosyncratic *meaning* of external events. His discovery that unconscious fantasy was powerfully able to blend itself with external reality to produce the alloy of psychic reality, capable itself of instigating hysteria, was his first clue to the importance of psychic reality in neurosis. His discovery that "there are no indications of reality in the unconscious" means that psychic reality, linked to unconscious fantasy, must be placed alongside external reality in his formulations.

Childhood sexual molestation was no longer rigidly required in the etiological formula. The indications that he had been getting from his patients that led him to surmise that they had been victims of a sexual assault, the memory of which was repressed, turned out to contain substantial doses of a wishful fantasy, also repressed. These fantasies had become connected to external events that were in themselves perhaps indifferent, leading to an experience of a sexual assault, which, although highly subjective, still had all the effect and appearance in the unconscious of an actual event.

Though he had lost his physical etiology and the hopes it had engendered, he had gained an appreciation of the power of spontaneous unconscious impulses and fantasies. Armed with this,

his assault of the problem of neurosis gained momentum. By February 1899, he could explain to Fliess how neurotic symptoms correspond even in their details to unconscious wishes. Unconscious fantasies were connected to wishes,[1] and the fantasy-wishes were expressions of impulses arising within the child.

The introduction of the element of unconscious fantasy into the equation had broadened the scientific scope of Freud's thinking by providing an explanation for two groups of patients who couldn't be fit into his physical model of hysteria. The first consisted of people who had been molested as children, but who managed *not* to develop hysteria (or other neuroses). This meant that an additional factor was apparently required for the occurrence of hysteria even in children who were molested. The only candidate available then was a kind of congenital brain damage, known at the time as "neuropathic taint." Freud found it impossible to believe that his lively and intelligent patients were so damaged, and vigorously defended them against what he regarded as a stigmatizing conjecture. The force of unconscious fantasy, mediating external events and giving them an idiosyncratic psychological significance, supplied the specific additional factor needed for hysteria to eventuate from a molestation.

A second group of cases for which his physical model offered no explanation was that of patients who develop hysteria without having been molested. His understanding of unconscious fantasy showed him that relatively innocuous external events could have the subjective significance of a sexual molestation.

Many years later in a brief autobiography (1925), Freud gave the following account of these developments:

> I must mention an error which I fell into and which might well have had fatal consequences for the whole of my work. Under the influence of the technical procedure which I used at that time [directing the patient's associations back to the locus of the hypothetical early memory], the majority of my patients reproduced from their childhood scenes in which they were sexually seduced by some grown-up person. With female patients the

---

[1]In the seventeenth century, "fantasy" meant wish or desire. The related word "fancy" still has this meaning.

part of the seducer was almost always assigned to their father. I believed these stories, and consequently supposed I had discovered the roots of the subsequent neurosis in these experiences of sexual seduction in childhood. My confidence was strengthened by a few, cases in which relations of this kind with a father, uncle or elder brother had continued up to an age at which memory was to be trusted. . . . When, however, I was at last obliged to recognize these scenes of seduction had never taken place, and that they were only phantasies which my patients had made up or which I myself had perhaps forced on them, I was for some time completely at a loss. My confidence alike in my technique and in its results were suffered a severe blow; it could not be disputed that I had arrived at these scenes by a technical method which I considered correct, and their subject-matter was unquestionably related to the symptoms from which my investigation had started. When I had pulled myself together, I was able to draw the right conclusions from my discovery; namely, that the neurotic symptoms were not related directly to actual events but to wishful phantasies, and that as far as the neurosis was concerned psychical reality was of more importance than material reality. . . .

It will be seen, then, that my mistake was of the same kind as would be made by someone who believed that the legendary story of the early kings of Rome (as told by Livy) was historical truth instead of what it is in fact — a reaction against the memory of times and circumstances which were insignificant and occasionally, perhaps, inglorious. [pp. 33–35]

Jones (1953) placed these developments into a nice perspective when he wrote that "irrespective of incest wishes of parents toward their children, and even of occasional acts of the kind, what [Freud] had to concern himself with [in his attempt to understand neurosis] was the general occurrence of incest wishes of children toward their parents" (p. 322). Freud was not rejecting the idea that children can be sexually traumatized by their parents, or that such traumas could be responsible for much pain and misery. He was merely pointing out that adults involving children in their sexual activities was not the *direct* cause of a neurosis and was not even required for one to develop. Another factor had to be taken into consideration: the spontaneous sexual wishes and fantasies of children themselves.

Infantile Sexuality

In March 1898, 18 months after he had given up the seduction theory, Freud wrote to Fliess that he was beginning to suspect that both dreams and neurotic symptoms stemmed from the "prehistoric period" of the patient's life, the period of childhood that cannot be remembered:

> The repetition of what was experienced in that period is in itself the fulfillment of a wish; a recent wish only leads to a dream if it can be put in connection with material from this period, if the recent wish is a derivative of a prehistoric wish or can get itself adopted by one. It is still an open question how far I shall be able to adhere to this extreme theory, or how far I can expose it to view in the dream book. [Freud 1985, p. 302]

The "dream book" is *The Interpretation of Dreams,* which he published two years later, and which he regarded throughout his life as his greatest achievement. It has "this extreme theory" as one of its foundations. Having recognized that the relevant phenomenon occurring in hysteria was not an early external event, but a particular type of interaction between a wishful fantasy and external events, Freud next asked under what conditions could this combination exert such power in the mind. He concluded that only fantasies that were expressions of powerful sexual impulses, already in force in the early childhood and infancy of his patients at the time when the "trauma" had occurred, would qualify.[2] These impulses endowed the fantasies with their ability to affect the mind in profound ways. Freud considered the sexual drive to be only one of a number of psychological drives, but his belief that neurotic patients came to grief only over their sexual impulses made him direct his attention to them.

Freud's theory of sexuality underwent many modifications during its career: The book in which he first expounded it, *Three*

---

[2]There was already at the time a considerable body of observation, collected as early as 1879 by pediatricians such as Lindner (1879), that supported the idea of spontaneous sexual impulses and activity in childhood.

Essays on the Theory of Sexuality (1905b), was revised six times, the last edition appearing in 1925. Its many editions make it too complex to treat in a summary form, and I shall therefore describe it here only in its early form, as it appeared circa 1905.

Freud considered sexual drives to arise from specific parts of the body known as erogenous zones—the mouth, the anus, and the genitals. Each zone gave rise spontaneously to its own type of sexual drive, and the force of each could be increased by stimulation of the appropriate erogenous zone (such as the "irritation of the genitals" that he had originally considered to provide the trauma that predisposes the child to hysteria). These drives produced tensions that demanded discharge.

For each type of sexual drive, Freud delineated a source, an aim, and an object. The source was the erogenous zone from which the drive arose. The aim was some activity that would bring about the discharge of the tension associated with the sexual impulse, and the object of the drive was some person or part of a person needed to bring about this discharge. For example, in the case of the oral drive, the source is the mouth, the aim is sucking, and the object is something to suck—a nipple or a thumb.

The Oedipus Complex

The sexual life of children is dominated first by one erogenous zone, then by another. The first zone to achieve dominance is the mouth, followed by the anus, and finally by the genitals. When the genital zone becomes dominant (which occurs at the age of 3 to 5 years), it brings the child into a triangular relationship, forcing it into a rivalry with one of its parents for sexual possession of the other—the Oedipus complex. To use the example of a little boy, he now takes his mother as the object of his genital impulses, and wishes to do something with her involving his genital. He recognizes that his father stands in the way of the fulfillment of this desire, and also is in some way able to obtain for himself the satisfaction denied to the boy. This causes him to hate the father whom he also loves, an extremely painful conflict. He then comes to fear the father who has now become his rival, and in particular to fear castration at the hands of the father. (The exact genesis of this fear was to remain obscure until about 1925, when Freud made the fundamental revision of his instinct theory considered in Chapter 9.) The conflict of the boy's simultaneous love, hatred, and fear of his father sets in motion the repression of the boy's genital desires for his mother, as a means of escaping the pain and anxiety.

A little girl's genital impulses would be directed toward her father, with the mother in the role of competitor. The explanation of the "repressed sexual molestation" Freud thought he had discovered was to be found in the unconscious wishful fantasies associated with the girl's oedipal impulses.

From this point of view, the crucial factor in the development of a neurosis is the magnitude of the clash between the child's sexual desires and the repressive forces operating within the child. Overly strong repression compounded by overly strong sexual desires would produce a violent derangement of sexual life, which presents itself many years later to the clinician as neurosis. Neurosis is therefore not the inevitable reaction of a mechanical system to the impact of an extraordinary external event, but one possible outcome of a child's mind struggling with the painful and universal advent of the Oedipus complex.

The Dynamic Unconscious

Freud's discovery that wishful fantasies played an essential role in the genesis of neurosis, that "as far as the neurosis was concerned, psychical reality was of more importance than material reality," was the first step in his recognition of the truly dynamic nature of the unconscious. His physical model of neurosis pictured the mind as a passive apparatus set in motion by external forces, and only to a very minor degree by forces arising from within itself. The series of discoveries of unconscious wishes, fantasies, and impulses that Freud grouped under the rubric of infantile sexuality drove him to conclude that the mind was also molded by forces that arose (and constantly arise) from within.

Moreover, by recognizing the impact of these unconscious, instinct-laden fantasies, with all their idiosyncratic variety, Freud found a way of accounting for the diversity of subjective individual responses to external events. When investigating how a psychological phenomenon might have arisen, he pictured to himself a continuum that he called an "etiologic series," along which was arrayed the range of possibilities, from a (hypothetical) pure fantasy experience unmixed with any realistic component, to the (equally hypothetical) pure external experience free of any element of fantasy. The instigator of a psychological event could lie at any point along the continuum except the extremes; what was important was not the impact of external reality or of internal impulse alone, but their sum.

Freud's ability to perceive the role of unconscious fantasy in the formation of neurotic symptoms and in the phenomenology of the consulting room, arose not only from his experiences with his patients but also from the analysis of himself that he was conducting concurrently. This took the form mainly of a study of his dreams, and it was for this purpose that he developed his characteristic psychoanalytic approach to psychological phenomena, by means of which he could begin to make out the unnoticed patterns of psychic reality that underlay the structure of dreams.

4

The Structure of Dreams and Neurosis

T hree years after his unpublished confession to Fliess that he could no longer maintain his physical theory of hysteria, Freud composed for publication an account of a case of hysteria he had just treated by a new method that, as a consequence of the insight into unconscious fantasy he had gained in the interval, had replaced cathartic treatment in his therapeutic armamentarium. The title of his account was "Fragment of an Analysis of a Case of Hysteria" (1905a), although it is more often referred to as the Dora case, after the pseudonym Freud gave his patient. It is the first report of the treatment of a patient by psychoanalysis.

In his preface to the report, Freud acknowledged the bewilderment its medical readers, used to thinking in terms of physical processes, were likely to experience. He explained that he had been driven in the course of his attempts to find a lasting cure for hysteria, into making a detailed examination of his patients' emotional lives. This had forced him to formulate a number of new ideas to account for his findings, quite unlike those with which his readers were familiar. Although this novel way of looking at hysteria had made sense out of certain of its hitherto mysterious aspects, he had arrived at it only at the price of loosening his mooring to the ground of physical processes with which medical science was familiar. Rather than apologizing for the distress this was likely to cause his readers, he boldly asserted that "in reality this bewildering character attaches to the phenomenon of the neurosis itself; its presence there is only concealed by the physician's familiarity with the [superficial] facts, and it comes to light again with every attempt to explain them" (p. 11). He went on to say that the sense of bewilderment

> could only be completely banished if we succeeded in tracing back every single element of a neurosis to factors with which we were already familiar. But everything tends to show that, on the contrary, we shall be driven by the study of neurosis to assume the existence of many new things which will [only] later on gradually become the subject of more certain knowledge. [1905a, p. 11]

Theories are good, but they don't prevent things from existing, and in case of conflict between theory and phenomena, it is the theory, not the phenomena, that needs alteration.

His boldness in standing free of the familiar physical medical models in his formulation of hysteria showed a Freud who was no longer the author of "Project for a Scientific Psychology." The medical traditionalist had given way to the clinical phenomenologist, and his interest in physical processes had become submerged in favor of the study of fantasy, wish, impulse, and emotion, which Freud now regarded — if not, perhaps, "equal in dignity to material processes" (as Helmholtz might have put it) — then at least as deserving of equal respect. The key to this transformation was his study of dreaming.

The Meaning of Dreams

Freud's interest in dreams extends back many years before the period we have been considering, at least to 1883 when he began keeping a notebook of his own dreams. At first, he regarded them, as he had hysteria, as epiphenomena of neural processes: Dream images were merely the mind's way of working out impressions that had registered during the day in some physical manner on the neural apparatus, but had not been "definitively dealt with" — that is, whose energy had not been completely discharged. The sleeping mind, he felt, was dominated by a "compulsion to link together any ideas which might be present in the same state of consciousness. The senseless and contradictory character of dreams could be traced back to the uncontrolled ascendancy of this latter factor" (Breuer and Freud 1895, p. 69n).

The nonsensical quality of dreams he supposed to be due to a physical charge that was associated with each dream idea, and that varied from one idea to another. Those ideas whose energy charge exceeded a threshold value would appear together in the dream, while others would not. From this point of view, dreams could have no more meaning than a tape recording cut to pieces and spliced back together in a random fashion. Ideas were linked together in dreams merely because they had happened to be present in the same undefined "state of consciousness," or happened to be laden with a large enough quota of energy. Since dreams had no meaning, they required no interpretation. The ideas and images appearing in them were the symptoms of an electrical relaxation of the brain, a sort of low-key electrical storm consisting of random discharges of built-up static energy.

His clinical contact with neurotic patients forced him to reexamine this view: He noticed that his patients would sometimes relate a dream as part of their account of the day's events, as though the dreams had a meaning comparable to the meaning of daytime thoughts. This apparently struck a chord in him, and he set out to see if dreams could be shown systematically to have psychological significance.

The task of finding how dreams fit into the rest of mental life occupied Freud for a number of years in the late 1890s. The fruit of his labors was a book published in 1900 entitled *Die Traumdeutung,* which is usually translated as "The Interpretation of Dreams" but which could, perhaps, be more accurately rendered as "The Meaning of Dreams." To the end of his long and extremely productive career (his psychological writings fill 23 volumes), he regarded *Die Traumdeutung* as his greatest achievement. An insight such as the one that produced the dream book, he said, was given to a man only once in a lifetime.

The index to *The Interpretation of Dreams* lists over 250 dreams, including about 50 of his own. The technique he adopted for fitting dreams into mental life consisted of focusing his attention loosely on each element of the dream in turn, noting what ideas occurred "of their own accord" — that is, without regard to their apparent relevance, importance, or logic — in connection with it. This approach, which he referred to as "keeping my critical faculty in abeyance," required a state of evenly suspended attention, withholding both criticism and deliberate attempts at interpretation until an interpretation "arose on its own" — took form, as it were, from the mass of associations itself.

Freud compared this to the attitude required for poetic creation, and quoted Schiller's response to a friend suffering from writer's block:

> The ground for your complaint seems to me to lie in the constraint imposed by your reason upon your imagination. I will make my idea more concrete by means of a simile. It seems a bad thing and detrimental to the creative work of the mind if Reason makes too close an examination of the ideas as they come pouring in — at the very gateway, as it were. Looked at in isolation, a thought may seem very trivial or very fantastic; but it may be made important by another thought that comes after it, and, in conjunction with other thoughts that may seem equally absurd, it may turn out to form a most effective link. Reason cannot form any opinion upon all this unless it retains the thought long enough to look at it in connection with the others. On the other hand, where there is a creative mind, Reason — so it seems to me — relaxes its watch upon the gates, and the ideas rush in pell-mell, and only then does it look them through and examine them in a mass. You critics, or whatever else you may call yourselves, are ashamed or frightened of the momentary and transient extravagances which are to be found in all truly creative minds and [only] whose longer or shorter duration distinguishes the thinking artist from the dreamer. You

complain of your unfruitfulness because you reject too soon and discriminate too severely. [1900, p. 103]

Charles Darwin put the matter less eloquently but more succinctly when he said that "it is fatal to reason whilst observing, though so necessary beforehand and so useful afterwards." The ability to look without preconceptions and without the need to rush to conclusions about what one is looking at is a state of mind whose value to the scientist Freud learned from Charcot. As Paul Valéry said, "to see is to forget the name of the thing one sees." The creative scientist and the creative artist share this ability to forget in order to see.

Freud regarded dream phenomena as Schiller had the "transient extravagances" of a creative mind. From such light-handed consideration of the elements of the dream, associations arose, and from them a meaning could be seen taking form. These associations seemed regularly to point to a wish, or rather to a fantasy that a wish the dreamer had harbored had come true in some magical way. The wish was one that would be painful for the dreamer to be aware of, since it would conflict with other, more conscious wishes, values, and desires. To avoid the pain of this conflict, the wish appeared in the dream in a disguised form. The dream forms a compromise between the unacceptable wish and the conflicting desire to suppress it, which means that the content of the dream is a partial expression of both conflicting tendencies, and a full expression of neither. The "irrational" character of dreams stems not from their being actually unrooted in any meaningful process, but from their being disguised, simultaneous expressions of incompatible ideas.

His theory of dreaming, as it emerged in *The Interpretation of Dreams,* posited not only an unconscious wish, but a force opposing its conscious expression that Freud called the "censorship." The unconscious fantasy that propelled the dream, in which an unacceptable wish was portrayed as magically fulfilled, was called the "latent content" of the dream, and the dream as it appears to the dreamer, after passing through the process of censorship, he called the "manifest content." Not all wishes were capable of causing a dream, but only those of the type he had referred to in his March 1898 letter to Fliess as "prehistoric wishes." These were related to

impulses from the period of infancy and childhood of which one has
no memory. The role of recent events, experiences, and wishes
(which, we recall, Freud had originally thought to be the sole
instigators of dreaming, by virtue of their having left impressions
that had not been discharged) was much reduced in the new theory.
Their importance consisted only in their suitability as vehicles
through which prehistoric wishes could be portrayed. As far as the
dream was concerned, they served as resonators for these ancient
impulses. The term Freud gave them was the "day residue."

Surprisingly, he was at a loss at first to explain why the wishes
contained in dreams had been censored and distorted. Although he
was aware by now from his clinical work that in neurosis, emotional
conflict had given rise to the repression of unconscious fantasies, and
that the effect of repression was to distort these fantasies into a
neurotic symptom, he failed at first to see the parallel between
dreaming and neurosis. Perhaps this was because at that point in his
investigations his thinking was still dominated by the idea that
repression was a pathological event found only in hysteria, an
electrical segmentation of the mental apparatus caused by a sexual
trauma in childhood. It would therefore not be found in normal
dreamers. He must have regarded the unconscious of the neurotic
and the unconscious revealed by dreams as two different species.

Dreams and Neurosis

When he dispensed with the theory that neurosis was the consequence of a physical trauma, Freud was free to see that repression
was not the consequence of a damaged mental apparatus, but that it
was also present in all dreamers. The unconscious of the neurotic
patient and that of the normal dreamer were therefore not as
different as he had supposed. He could then conceive of the whole of
neurosis in terms of dreams. He arrived at this juncture as a result
of having seen that psychic reality, an alloy of external events and
unconscious fantasy, was the operative level of events in both
phenomena.

In this light, dreams and neurosis shared a common structure.
Corresponding to the conflict between wish and censorship in

dreaming was that between infantile sexual impulse and repression in neurosis. Unconscious fantasy stood in relation to neurotic symptoms in neurosis as the latent content of the dream to its manifest content. Finally, the external event that precipitates the outbreak of a neurosis, an experience congruent enough with a powerful unconscious fantasy to become the stimulus for its expression in the form of symptomatology, corresponded to the day residue.

Dreams and neurotic symptoms shared this structure because they were simply different expressions of repressed wishes. Freud called the idea that dreams were disguised wish-fulfillments his "psychological theory," to contrast it with the physiological, or trauma, theory of his earlier writings. When the trauma theory became untenable, he wrote to Fliess, paraphrasing Nietzsche, that "in the collapse of all values only the psychological theory has remained unimpaired. The theory of dreams stands as sure as ever." Having been forced to return to his psychological theory, he found there the structural links between dreaming and neurosis that enabled him to reemerge with a new theory of neurosis built on his theory of dreams. Dreams, as he had said, *did* contain the psychology of neurosis in a nutshell. In the symptoms of neurosis and in the manifest content of dreams, the same wishful fantasies could be found, distorted in the same way by the same force of repression.

Repression

Like the notion of unconscious fantasy, repression was not an a priori theoretical construct, but a discovery arising out of attention to clinical phenomena. When Freud was still using the cathartic method to treat hysteria, he found that when he attempted to get his patients to recall the events surrounding the appearance of their hysterical symptoms, they were unable to remember certain of them. He realized that

> everything that had been forgotten had in some way or other been distressing. . . . It was impossible not to conclude that this was precisely why it had been forgotten — that is, why it had not

remained conscious. In order to make it conscious again in spite
of this, it was necessary to overcome something that fought
against one in the patient. . . . The amount of effort required of
the physician varied in different cases; it increased in direct
proportion to the difficulty of what had to be remembered. The
expenditure of force on the part of the physician was evidently
the measure of a *resistance* on the part of the patient. It was only
necessary to translate into words what I had observed and I was
in possession of the theory of *repression*. [1925, p. 29]

While Freud was not the first to arrive at the idea of an
unconscious — that parts of the mind exist that are inaccessible to
consciousness — he was the first to take seriously the idea that its
inaccessibility could be the result of emotional forces that opposed
its entry into consciousness. The idea that repression is due to
emotional forces distinguishes the psychoanalytic conception of the
unconscious from other notions of it.

It is important to see that resistance is not the same as
disagreement with what the analyst happens to say to the patient.
The analyst's interpretation may in fact be incorrect, and the
patient's so-called resistance is therefore justified. A patient may
demonstrate his or her commitment to finding the truth equally well
by disagreeing with the analyst as by agreeing. Freud conveys this
point in an anecdote: As he was watching the hypnotist Bernheim
work with one of his patients, he recalled feeling a

muffled hostility to this tyranny of suggestion. When a patient
who showed himself unamenable was met with the shout: "What
are you doing? *Vous vous contre-suggestionnez!*", I said to myself that
this was an evident injustice and an act of violence. For the man
certainly had a right to counter-suggestions if people were trying
to subdue him with suggestions. [1921, p. 89]

Resistance in its true sense means resistance to the *process* of
analysis, whereby the patient does not confirm, deny, or associate
further to an interpretation, but more or less opts out of the
interchange with the analyst. This opting out is, as a rule, involun-
tary, and is often the result of an unconscious fantasy operating
within the patient that prevents further cooperation. When the
patient understands this fantasy, the analysis can proceed.

Freud called his concept of the unconscious the "dynamic unconscious"; he chose this term to emphasize that it is an area of the mind actively and continuously cut off from consciousness by emotional *forces*. Just as repressed unconscious wishes are driven by emotions (derived ultimately from instinctual drives), so repression is also driven by the force of emotion. Freud himself dated the birth of psychoanalysis from the recognition of this emotional significance of repression:

The theory of repression became the cornerstone of our understanding of neurosis. A different view now had to be taken of the task of therapy. Its aim was no longer to "abreact" an affect which had got on to the wrong lines but to uncover repressions and replace them by acts of judgement which might result either in the accepting or in the condemning of what had formerly been repudiated. I showed my recognition of the new situation by no longer calling my method of investigation and treatment *catharsis* but *psycho-analysis*. [1925, p. 30]

5

Transference and the Crystallization of the Psychoanalytic Method

The Role of Transference in Psychoanalysis

Freud considered his treatment of Dora to be the first example of a psychoanalysis because it was the first in which he applied to neurotic symptomatology the approach he had developed to investigate the meaning of dreams. He found that it was as effective in illuminating the meaning of neurosis as it had been with dreams. This was no accident, but a consequence of the common origin of dreams and neurosis in the dynamic process of repression. Like dreams, neurotic symptoms had a psychological meaning, were propelled by the force of unconscious emotion, and were represented by disguised expressions of repressed "prehistoric wishes," by which, at this point in his theoretical development, Freud meant infantile sexual impulses.

In the course of her analysis, Dora told Freud two dreams that he was able to trace back to the same repressed wishes that had given

rise to her neurotic symptoms. He was delighted to have demonstrated in an actual case the link he suspected between these two
disparate phenomena, and for this reason he decided to publish it.
He gave the draft of his case report the title "Dreams and Hysteria."

But just when the analysis appeared to be progressing toward a
satisfactory resolution, Dora abruptly broke it off, never to return.
Freud commemorated this event by changing the title of his report
to "Fragment of an Analysis of a Case of Hysteria." In addition to
the point he wished this case to make, "Dora" turned out to contain
another he had not anticipated: Repressed impulses express themselves not only in dreams and neurotic symptoms, but also in the
form of a new phenomenon, the transference, a fact Freud appre-
ciated only too late. Dora's breaking off her analysis was a manifestation of her transference. He may have been thinking of her when
he later said that every advance in psychoanalysis is achieved only at
the cost of a failed treatment.

In order to understand the nature of the transference, we must
review the way in which it emerged during Dora's analysis. She was
an 18-year-old girl who was brought to Freud by her father for
treatment. For some time, she had suffered from a hysterical
neurosis manifested by shortness of breath, long bouts of coughing,
and fainting. The part of Dora's story that drove home the lesson of
the transference was not connected to her symptoms but to a certain
quality in the relationships she formed with people she loved.

"Dora" is a good illustration of Freud's observation that his case
histories read more like novellas than scientific accounts. Her father
had brought her to Freud not entirely because of his concern over
her symptoms, but because he was worried about her well-grounded
suspicions that he had been having an affair with a family friend,
Frau K. Dora was in turn strongly attracted to Frau K.'s young and
handsome husband, a fact which had not escaped her father's notice,
and of which he approved inasmuch as he felt it would ally Dora to
him in his liason with Frau K. Dora was at least half aware that her
father was in favor of her romantic learnings toward Herr K. One
day, while the two families were vacationing together at a lake, Herr
K. pressed his suit with Dora, who reacted not like a young girl in
love whose dreams had come true (as might have been expected),
but by slapping Herr K.'s face and developing a violent and genuine
hatred of him.

Into this Victorian family drama strode Freud, eager for an opportunity to put into practice his new approach to neurosis. He managed to piece together the circumstances of Dora's complex emotional life partly from her own account and partly from his interpretations of her dreams. In doing so, he caught a glimpse of something that Dora was not aware of: Dora identified Herr K. with her father in a number of ways, and her erotic attraction to him led back in Dora's associations to an earlier one toward her father.

To add to the complexity, Dora's romance with Herr K. had been preceded a few years earlier by an even more passionate one with Frau K., so that when Dora began to suspect the real nature of Frau K.'s relationship with her father, she felt betrayed not as much by him as by her. She had then turned to Herr K. partly out of a wish for vengeance against Frau K., a wish motivated not only by the immediate and realistic disappointment, but by an old one as well: In childhood, Dora had been single-mindedly attached to her own mother and, finding that the feeling was not completely mutual, turned to her father out of spite. Her relationship with both of the K.'s was also a repetition of the infantile triangle in which Dora had found herself with her parents, and which was somehow being kept alive through Dora's relationship with them.

This layering of relationships and attachments back in time — each later layer inheriting from the earlier ones forgotten ties of love, hate, jealousy, and spite — reflected the mode of operation of the unconscious with which Freud was already familiar from his study of dreams. Dora's relationship with the K.'s was formed like a dream element: A current wish provided a vehicle for a still-vital infantile wish, enabling the former to serve as a present-day modus vivendi of the latter.

After interpreting the second of the two dreams that had provided the key to Dora's neurotic symptoms, Freud allowed himself an expression of satisfaction with his work. But Dora, he writes,

> replied in a depreciatory tone: "Why, has anything so very remarkable come out?" These words prepared me for the advent of fresh revelations.
>
> She opened the [next] session with these words: "Do you know that I am here for the last time today?"–"How can I know, as you have said nothing to me about it?" — "Yes. I made

up my mind to put up with it until the New Year [it was December 31st]. But I shall wait no longer than that to be cured."–"You know that you are free to stop the treatment at any time. But for today we will go on with our work. When did you come to this decision?"–"A fortnight ago, I think."–"That sounds just like a maidservant or a governess — a fortnight's warning-."–"There was a governess who gave warning with the K.'s, when I was on my visit to them that time at L＿＿＿ , by the lake."–"Really? You never told me about her. Tell me." [1905a, p. 105]

Dora said that she had been told by the K.'s governess, a few days before the scene at the lake, that Herr K. had made a sexual advance toward her, telling her that he got nothing from his wife.

"Why, those are the very words he used afterwards, when he made his proposal to you and when you gave him a slap in his face."–"Yes. She had given way to him, but after a little while he had ceased to care for her, and since then she hated him. . . ."
    Here therefore (and quite in accordance with the rules) was a piece of information coming to light in the middle of an analysis and helping to solve problems which had previously been raised. I was able to say to Dora: "Now I know your motive for the slap in the face with which you answered Herr K.'s proposal. It was not that you were offended at his suggestions; you were actuated by jealousy and revenge. At the time when the governess was telling you her story you were still able to make use of your gift for putting on one side everything that is not agreeable to your feelings. But at the moment when Herr K. used the words 'I get nothing from my wife' — which were the same words he had used to the governess — fresh emotions were aroused in you and tipped the balance. 'Does he dare,' you said to yourself, 'to treat me like a governess, like a servant?' Wounded pride added to jealousy and to the conscious motives of common sense — it was too much." [1905a, p. 106]

At this point it emerged for the first time that Dora had been quite seriously entertaining the idea of Herr K. divorcing his wife and marrying her. The report continues:

Dora listened to me without any of her usual contradictions. She seemed to be moved; she said good-bye to me very warmly, with the heartiest wishes for the New Year, and — came no more. Her father, who called on me two or three times afterwards, assured me that she would come back again, and said it was easy to see that she was eager for the treatment to continue. But it must be confessed that Dora's father was never entirely straightforward. . . . I knew Dora would not come back again. Her breaking off so unexpectedly, just when my hopes of a successful termination of the treatment were at their highest, and her thus bringing those hopes to nothing — this was an unmistakable act of vengeance on her part. Her purpose of self-injury also profited by this action. No one who, like me, conjures up the most evil of those half-tamed demons that inhabit the human breast, and seeks to wrestle with them, can expect to come through the struggle unscathed. Might I perhaps have kept the girl under my treatment if I myself had acted a part, if I had exaggerated the importance to me of her staying on, and had shown a warm personal interest in her — a course which, even after allowing for my position as her physician, would have been tantamount to providing her with a substitute for the affection she longed for? I do not know. Since in every case a portion of the factors that are encountered under the form of resistance remains unknown, I have always avoided acting a part, and have contented myself with practicing the humbler acts of psychology. In spite of every theoretical interest and of every endeavor to be of assistance as a physician, I keep the fact in mind that there must be some limits set to the extent to which psychological influence may be used, and I respect as one of these limits the patient's own will and understanding. [1905a, pp. 108–109]

Dora had exacted her revenge by dashing Freud's hopes just at the moment he had conveyed them to her by his expression of satisfaction at the progress of the analysis, exactly as her hopes and pride had been dashed by Herr K., who was himself only the latest in a long series of loves, reaching back into her childhood, by whom she had felt betrayed. She had turned the table, placing herself in the position of Herr K. (and his antecedents in her life), and placing Freud in the position she had been in with them. But by this time, Herr K. was no longer the latest in Dora's chain of unrequited loves: Freud himself was.

In the transference, Freud had been added to Dora's personal historical romantic series that began in childhood with her mother, followed by her father, Frau K., and finally, Herr K. In his postscript to the Dora case, Freud elaborates on his new discovery:

> What are the transferences? They are . . . a whole series of [past] psychological experiences [that] are revived, not as belonging to the past, but as applying to the person of the physician at the present moment. Some of these transferences have a content which differs from that of their model in no respect whatever except for the substitution. . . . Others are more ingeniously constructed; their content has been subjected to a moderating influence . . . and they may even become conscious, by cleverly taking advantage of some real peculiarity in the physician's person or circumstances and attaching themselves to that. [1905a, p. 116]

The transference is driven by unconscious fantasies in which the relationship between the patient and the analyst is portrayed in terms other than what it actually is: two people meeting together for the purpose of psychoanalysis. So individual is the aggregate character of these unconscious fantasies that, in an analysis, the fully developed transference constitutes a unique psychological fingerprint.

Freud goes on to consider the implications of his discovery for psychoanalysis:

> If the theory of analytic technique is gone into, it becomes evident that transference is an inevitable necessity. Practical experience, at all events, shows conclusively that there is no means of avoiding it, and that this latest creation of the disease must be combatted like all the earlier ones. This happens, however, to be by far the hardest part of the whole task. . . . Nevertheless, transference cannot be evaded, since use of it is made in setting up all the obstacles that make the material inaccessible to treatment, and since it is only after the transference has been resolved that a patient arrives at a sense of conviction of the validity of the connections which have been constructed during the analysis. . . .
>
> The physician's labors are not multiplied by transference; it need make no difference to him whether he has to overcome any particular impulse of the patient's in connection with himself or

with someone else. Nor does the treatment force upon the patient, in the shape of transference, any new task he would not have otherwise performed. It is true that neuroses may be cured in institutions from which psycho-analytic treatment is excluded, that hysteria may be said to be cured not by the method but by the physician, and that there is usually a sort of blind dependence and a permanent bond between a patient and a physician who has removed his symptoms by hypnotic suggestion; but the scientific explanation of these facts is to be found in the existence of "transferences" such as are regularly directed by patients to their physicians. Psychoanalytic treatment does not *create* transferences, it merely brings them to light, like so many other hidden psychical factors. [1905a, p. 116]

Later, he observed that

in institutions in which nerve patients are treated non-analytically, we can observe transference occurring with the greatest intensity and in the most unworthy forms, extending to nothing less than mental bondage, and moreover showing the plainest erotic coloring. . . . These characteristics of transference are therefore to be attributed not to psycho-analysis but to neurosis itself. [1912, p. 101]

What distinguishes psychoanalysis from nonanalytic psychotherapies is not the occurrence of transference but the response of the analyst to it. In nonanalytic treatments, where the "hysteria may be said to be cured not by the method but by the physician," the physician makes use of the transference to influence the patient in the direction of behaving and feeling in what is regarded as a more normal fashion.

In psycho-analysis on the other hand, since the play of [the physician's] motives is different, all the patient's tendencies, including hostile ones, are aroused; they are then turned to account for the purpose of the analysis by being made conscious, and in this way the transference is continually being destroyed. [1905a, p. 117]

In psychoanalysis, all of the transferred feelings, both positive and negative, are to be dealt with even-handedly; the analyst does not cultivate the positive transference nor evade the negative one.

Freud realized that he might have avoided the interruption of Dora's analysis if he had played into the transference by gratifying her wish to be treated as more than a patient. But he also recognized that even though doing so would enable him to avoid a confrontation with the "half-tamed demon" of her jealous rage, it would also obscure an important part of Dora's mind whose illumination, it was clear in retrospect, was the whole point of the analysis. He decided that for the sake of the analysis, the transference must neither be ignored, as he had done, nor played into, but *interpreted* in the same way as any other manifestation of the patient's unconscious world.

Freud reasoned that when the therapist acts the role that the transference has specified for him in order to gain emotional leverage over the patient, as in supportive psychotherapies, the patient never becomes aware that an unconscious fantasy produces the transference, because it has become obscured by the reality of the therapist's behavior. Therefore, no integration of it into consciousness is possible.

When the analyst refrains from acting this part, the ensuing bad fit between the patient's unconscious fantasy and the external reality produces a kind of emotional turbulence, a sign that the forces underlying the transference are beginning to enter consciousness. The analyst may then draw the patient's attention to them by means of an interpretation.

The great importance of the transference in psychoanalysis lies in its unique epistemological role. When a patient reports past or present experiences with a spouse, sibling, or parent, the analyst, who is not omniscient, can only defer to the patient's long experience with people the analyst has perhaps never even met. When the patient's experience of the analyst himself is at issue, the analyst is in a position to make an independent assessment, since he has himself had the opportunity to observe first hand *all* the events that have gone into forming the patient's experience of him. Or rather, he has observed all the relevant events external to the patient. This enables him to infer with a relatively high degree of certainty the contribution that internal events have made to the patient's overall experience of the analyst. The sense of conviction about these internal events that both analyst and patient may thus arrive at is unparalleled in any other type of interpretation.

This is what Freud had in mind when he wrote that

> transference, which seems ordained to be the greatest obstacle to psycho-analysis, becomes its most powerful ally, if its presence can be detected each time and explained to the patient. [1905a, p. 117]

By refraining from acting a part and confining himself to simply looking, the psychoanalyst makes transference visible. Analysis acts like a microscope that enables the analyst to see forms of life that are present everywhere, but impossible to see under ordinary conditions.

The analyst's interpretation of the transference also has the effect of encouraging the patient to focus further transferences on him, a phenomenon Meltzer (1967) has called the "gathering of the transference" in the analysis. It is as though the patient experienced the analyst's interpretive activity as a haven for the transferences that have been occupying (and interfering with) various parts of his life, and uses the opportunity of analysis to secure more of them in a safe place. The analyst's role in regard to the transference is merely to "hold" it, to be willing to bear whatever transference significance the patient assigns him, to describe the assignment, and to investigate the reasons for it.

The Crystallization of the Psychoanalytic Method

Like dreams and neurosis, transference represented the use by an unconscious infantile impulse of a suitable situation in the external world as a vehicle for its expression, giving the situation an idiosyncratic psychological significance. Also like dreams and neurosis, it represented the force of repression that allowed the impulse only partial expression, and it operated largely underground, so that the final product appeared to have sprung forth without reason. With the discovery that transference was a product of the same kind of transformations as dreams and neurosis, motivated by the same dynamics, and analyzable in the same way, Freud could place it alongside them in a general class of phenomena of which dreaming stood as the prototype. The underlying order that unified the three was now evident.

Free Association

Since dreams, neurosis, and transference were each creations of unconscious processes, Freud had in his possession three separate routes into the unconscious. The means by which these routes were traversed in clinical practice was a technical procedure Freud evolved for conducting an analysis, which he called *free association*. In German, the term is *freier Einfall,* which can also be translated as "free intrusion," a translation that better conveys the idea that what he was after was a technique that would allow traces of the unconscious to penetrate as much as possible against omnipresent resistance into consciousness.

The technique of free association is an outgrowth of Freud's method of ferreting out the unconscious elements contributing to the formation of his dreams. There, we recall, he would think of each element of the dream he was trying to analyze with evenly suspended attention, observing as impartially as he could what intruded into his mind in connection with it. He made no conscious effort to associate to the dream elements, but merely let into his mind whatever appeared to well up of its own accord.

He extended this approach to the clinical setting of psychoanalysis by encouraging his patients to adopt the state of mind he had himself found essential for exploring the unconscious. He told them to communicate to him whatever came to mind at the moment, what followed that, and so on, without any conscious censorship or editing whatsoever. He wanted them to relax their "critical faculties" for the sake of being able to observe their own states of mind and to report on them as freely as they could. He believed that some surface of the unconscious is always presenting itself to consciousness, and if premature closure could be avoided, something can be learned about it from the imprint it makes on conscious states of mind.

Of course, free association cannot really be done freely. Qualms, reservations, blocks, and the desire for a superficial explanation and rapid closure always creep into our attempts to observe candidly our own states of mind. Resistance interferes with our contact with even the nearest surface of the unconscious; however, resistance is also, paradoxically, indispensable to the success of analysis. Without resistance, it would not be possible to know when one was in the vicinity of an unconscious determinant of a dream, idea, or symptom. The reason for this is that any idea or fantasy that is unconscious in the dynamic sense is (by definition) repressed by emotional forces. Since resistance is the clinical manifestation of repression, it is only where it appears that analysis—the discovery of new meaning—can take place.

Freud's use of free association and resistance for fathoming unconscious meaning is concisely illustrated in the following analysis of an instance of symptomatic forgetting.

Last summer . . . I renewed my acquaintance with a certain young man of academic background. I soon found that he was familiar with some of my psychological publications. We had fallen into conversation—how I have now forgotten—about the social status of the race to which we both belonged; and ambitious feelings prompted him to give vent to a regret that his generation was doomed (as he expressed it) to atrophy, and could not develop its talents or satisfy its needs. He ended a speech of impassioned fervor with the well-known line of Virgil's in which the unhappy Dido commits to posterity her vengeance on Aeneas: *"Exoriare. . . ."* Or rather, he *wanted* to end it in this way, for he could not get hold of the quotation and tried to conceal an obvious gap in what he remembered by changing the order of the words: *"Exoriar(e) ex nostris ossibus ultor."* At last he said irritably: "Please don't look so scornful: you seem as if you were gloating over my embarrassment. Why not help me? There's something missing in the line; how does the whole thing really go?"

"I'll help you with pleasure," I replied, and gave the quotation in its correct form: *"Exoriare ALIQUIS nostris ex ossibus ultor"* [Let someone arise from my bones as an avenger].

"How stupid of me to forget a word like that! By the way, you claim that one never forgets a thing without some reason. I should be very curious to learn how I came to forget the indefinite pronoun *'aliquis'* in this case."

I took up his challenge most readily, for I was hoping for a contribution to my collection [of mental slips]. So I said, "That should not take us long. I must only ask you to tell me, *candidly* and *uncritically,* whatever comes into your mind if you direct your attention to the forgotten word without any definite aim."

"Good. There springs to my mind, then, the ridiculous notion of dividing up the word like this: *a* and *liquis.*"

"What does that mean?" "I don't know." "And what occurs to you next?" "What comes next is *Reliquien* [relics], *liquifying, fluidity, fluid.* Have you discovered anything so far?"

"No. Not by any means yet. But go on."

"I am thinking," he went on with a scornful laugh, "of *Simon of Trent,* whose relics I saw two years ago in a church at Trent. I am thinking of the accusation of ritual blood-sacrifice which is being brought against the Jews again just now, and of *Kleinpaul's* book in which he regards all these supposed victims as incarnations, one might say new editions, of the Saviour."

"The notion is not entirely unrelated to the one we were discussing before the Latin word slipped your memory."

"True. My next thoughts are about an article I read lately in an Italian newspaper. Its title, I think, was 'What St. *Augustine* says about women.' What do you make of that?"

"I am waiting."

"And now comes something that is clearly unconnected with our subject."

"Please refrain from any criticism and—"

"Yes, I understand. I am thinking of a fine old gentleman I met on my travels last week. He was a real *original,* with all the appearance of a huge bird of prey. His name was *Benedict,* if it's of interest to you."

"Anyhow, here are a row of saints and Fathers of the Church: St. *Simon,* St. *Augustine,* St. *Benedict.* There was, I think, a Church Father called *Origen.* Moreover, three of these names are also first names, like *Paul* in Kleinpaul."

"Now it's St. *Januarius* and the miracle of the blood that comes into my mind—my thoughts seem to be running on mechanically."

"Just a moment: St. *Januarius* and St. *Augustine* both have to do with the calendar. But won't you remind me about the miracle of his blood?"

"Surely you must have heard of that? They keep the blood of St. Januarius in a phial inside a church at Naples, and on a particular holy day it miraculously *liquifies*. The people attach great importance to this miracle and get very excited if it's delayed, as happened once at a time when the French were occupying the town. So the general in command — or have I got it wrong? — was it Garibaldi? — took the reverend gentleman aside and gave him to understand, with an unmistakable gesture towards the soldiers posted outside, that he *hoped* the miracle would take place very soon. And in fact it did take place. . . ."

"Well, go on. Why do you pause?"

"Well, something *has* come into my mind . . . but it's too intimate to pass on. . . . Besides, I don't see any connection, or any necessity for saying it."

"You can leave the connection to me. Of course, I can't force you to talk about something that you find distasteful; but then you musn't insist on learning from me how you came to forget your *aliquis*."

"Really? Is that what you think? Well then, I've suddenly thought of a lady from whom I might easily hear a piece of news that would be very awkward for both of us."

"That her periods have stopped?"

"How could you guess that?"

"That's not difficult any longer; you've prepared the way sufficiently. Think of the *calendar saints, the blood that starts to flow on a particular day, the disturbance when the event fails to take place, the open threats that the miracle must be vouchsafed, or else.* . . . In fact, you've made use of the miracle of St. Januarius to manufacture a brilliant allusion to women's periods."

"Without being aware of it. And you really mean to say that it was this anxious expectation that made me unable to produce an unimportant word like *aliquis*?"

"It seems to me undeniable. You need only recall the division you made into *a-liquis,* and your associations: *relics, liquifying, fluid.* St. Simon was *sacrificed as a child* — shall I go on and show how he comes in? You were led on to him by the subject of relics."

"No, I'd much rather you didn't. I hope you don't take these thoughts of mine too seriously, if indeed I really had them. In return I will confess to you that the lady is Italian and that I went to Naples with her. But mayn't this all be just a matter of chance?"

"I must leave it to your own judgement to decide whether you
can explain all these connections on the assumption that they are
matters of chance. I can however tell you that every case like this
that you care to analyse will lead you to 'matters of chance' that
are just as striking." [1901, pp. 8–11]

Free-Floating Attention

The analyst's counterpart to free association is what Freud called
"free-floating attention." Again, the salient model is the kind of
contact with the unconscious provided by the analysis of dreams.
In psychoanalysis the analyst must be in contact with the patient's
unconscious, which means he must stand in relation to the patient as
he does to himself when analyzing his own dreams. He must
therefore arrive at the same open, relaxed but attentive state that
Freud had first summoned up for the purpose of analyzing his own
dreams. This state may also be described as reverie or musing.
Freud once wrote that during the analysis the analyst must create a
beam of darkness, artificially blinding himself to the apparent and
"reasonable" so that its glare doesn't wash out the still shadowy
pattern of the patient's unconscious. Like a dreamer, he must
withdraw from the glare of the outer world in order to make out the
muted tracings of the inner one. Unlike a dreamer, the analyst must
maintain contact with the unconscious of someone else.

This state of mind—the capacity to look in a certain way at
one's own or another's mind—is the essence of psychoanalytic
contact. This is why the core of an analyst's training consists of being
psychoanalyzed himself. His own analysis gives him a means of
establishing a rapport with his own unconscious and through that,
with the patient's. The physical and temporal structure of the
psychoanalytic session, the analyst's behavior, and so on, are
expedients whose sole legitimate purpose is to produce optimal
conditions for psychoanalytic contact.

Using the approach to dreams he developed in the mid-1890s,
Freud could not perceive the psychic realities underlying such
diverse phenomena as neurosis, dreaming, transference, resistance,
and unintentional slips. He recognized that transference and resis-

tance are indicators of unconscious psychic reality that are particularly important to the practical epistemologic task of identifying unconscious states of mind, because they manifest themselves vividly and directly in the immediate experience of the analytic session. He could now characterize psychoanalysis quite succinctly, on methodological grounds alone, as a way of exploring transference and resistance, a discipline within which any theory could be entertained that seemed to do justice to the phenomena whose existence the exploration revealed.

6

Gravitational Confinement

T he four years separating Freud's letter to Fliess heralding the death of the seduction theory, and his discovery of the transference, witnessed the transformation of an ambitious young neurologist eager to establish himself as a master of the as-yet unclaimed disease of hysteria into a percipient observer of the phenomenology of the mind. During this period, Freud discovered psychoanalysis in all its essentials, the structure of which may at this point be pictured as a pyramid. Its base is a way of looking at states of mind—originated in an attempt to find meaning in dreams, and refined in the psychoanalytic treatment of neurosis—that suffers unexplained and unfamiliar details to exist unmolested long enough for their own patterns to emerge. This is psychoanalytic contact. Resting on this are the psychoanalytic setting and technique, dictated by the practical requirements for seeing the flickers of the unconscious in the obscuring glare of resistance and conscious mental activities.

Finally, at the apex are the various models and theories which are attempts at shorthand description of the phenomena seen in the psychoanalytic setting.

Among the reaches covered by these new psychoanalytic models was that of the etiology of neurosis, left open by the collapse of Freud's seduction theory of hysteria. His new model differed radically from the one it replaced: The cause of neurosis was not simply the weight of external events burdening a mental apparatus to the breaking point, as an electrical overload might burn out a delicate piece of electronic equipment. Instead, a neurosis develops when external events come to resemble too closely certain unconscious impulses and fantasies, which tend to meet such events at least halfway. These unconscious fantasies, located in the domain of psychic reality, then acquire a power over the mind that they cannot have when external realities do not conform to them so closely. It is the readiness of one's unconscious fantasies to join suitable external events that predisposes one to falling ill under the impact of events, and it is the meaning of the resulting subjective experiences that triggers a neurosis.

The object of the psychoanalytic search was now to find what unconscious impulse had joined to what external event, and how the joining had affected the significance of the event—that is, how its meaning had been transformed during its passage from external reality to unconscious psychic reality. The main clinical approaches to these phenomena were the psychoanalytic study of dreams, neurotic symptoms, and, above all, transference and resistance. Furthermore, the forces maintaining a neurosis were not events that had occurred in the remote past, the impact of which had not been sufficiently discharged, but ongoing unconscious psychic realities, manifestations in part of infantile parts of the mind that were still alive, exerting their dynamic effect on one's interpretation of events. The focus of investigation, therefore, shifted from the past to the present—that is, from tracking down forgotten external events of childhood that supposedly lay pressing on the mind like an abscess, to identifying certain facts about present-day unconscious psychic reality, most especially in its clearest manifestation, the transference.

The Persistence of Freud's Original Model

In order to present a more coherent picture of the nature of Freud's transformation, I have made it seem sharper and more monotonic than it actually was. In reality, Freud never entirely abandoned his original model of neurosis as a physical process. He had indeed become a phenomenologist looking at the details of psychic reality in a new way, in a new setting, and formulating what he saw in terms of models containing "many new things." But he also remained a physician clinging to the vast, impressive, and, above all, familiar tradition of nineteenth-century physical medicine in which he had been trained. From that point of view the new models of repression, transference, unconscious fantasy, and dreaming—the fruits of his psychoanalytic perceptions—were merely intermediate stages, or even at times unwelcome detours, on the road to his ultimate Helmholtzian goal, a model of the mind that contained only terms readily "reducible to the forces of attraction and repulsion."

One can thus find running through much of Freud's work, especially in the higher-level theorizing of what he called his "metapsychology," a wistful tendency to regard psychology as a kind of physics and to treat emotions, ideas, and states of mind in general as epiphenomenal expressions of the energic state of the mental apparatus. Freud's boldness in exploring territories so new that he had to invent his own navigational equipment as he went along was laced through with a determination to claim sightings of the homeland, and so end his explorations by making a premature closure between his current position and the relative safety of physical science.

This tendency toward premature closure with what is familiar is most evident in his theory of libido. Freud's sexual theory, as expressed in "Three Essays on the Theory of Sexuality," was really two distinct theories. The first was a psychological one, his theory of infantile sexuality proper, which held that sexual life begins before adolescence, and that there is a genetic continuity between infantile (childhood) sexuality on one hand and adult perversions and normal adult sexuality on the other. His theory of neurosis rested in part on infantile sexuality, which provided the motives, in the form of persistent infantile sexual wishes, necessary to drive one side of the conflict of which the neurosis was an expression. Freud's theory of infantile sexuality was based on first-hand clinical observations, such as Lindner's (1879), of children's sexual activities, and on the fantasies that he himself uncovered in the consulting room.

The Theory of Libido

The second theory was his theory of libido. "Libido" is the name he gave to a hypothetical physical fluid emanating from the erogenous zones of the body (mouth, anus, and genitals), which provided the physical energy to drive the mental apparatus. It was released from these zones automatically and continuously at a baseline rate, although the level of libido in the system could be increased by physical stimulation of the zones. As a fluid, it could flow through the physical and mental apparatus, be stored in various places, and, if one of its pathways was blocked, could back up and flow along a secondary path. It produced a psychological tension that was the same regardless of its anatomical source.

Freud considered the various erogenous zones to be interconnected by "collateral channels." If discharge of libido was blocked at one channel, it could "regress" — that is, it could flow backward and eventually emerge through another channel associated with a different erogenous zone, a process that changed its character to correspond to the new channel. For example, genital libido that could not be discharged would be transformed in this way to oral or anal libido, and it was these more primitive forms of libido that in turn gave rise to the symptoms of neurosis.

Now, Freud's psychological theory of infantile sexuality may be formulated in its entirety without reference to libido. This is how modern psychoanalytic theories of sexuality are in fact formulated; but it has taken the better part of a century for psychoanalysts to divest themselves completely of the legacy of libido theory, the last bastion having given way only in the last few years in the United States. The theory of libido stands in the same relation to the psychology of infantile sexuality as the physiology of the "Project for a Scientific Psychology" stands in relation to Freud's psychological theory of dreaming.

Freud seems to have introduced the hypothesis of libido only as a way of accounting for the development of sexual life and neurosis in terms with which he and his physician colleagues would feel more comfortable. He could do so because libido itself is simply a version of the electrical fluid he assumed to be the cause of the symptoms of hysteria, before he discovered that they could be motivated by unconscious fantasy. His retreat back to an electrical fluid served to blur, in his own eyes as well as others', the novelty of what he had discovered about psychic reality, a blurring that shows itself in the ambiguousness of his language in this area. For example, "libido" is a form of the Latin word for "desire," and when he wrote of an object becoming filled with libido, he seems to mean that it had become an object of desire, and hence of psychological significance. The ebb and flow of libido seems to be a way of speaking about the waxing and waning of desire, and the discharge of libido the extinguishing (or satisfaction) of desire. But he uses the same term to refer to material events of the kind he had in mind when he wrote in 1894 of "an electric charge" distributed throughout a system. This use of terms to refer to both psychological and material events without distinguishing one from the other suggests that the psychological phenomena he had discovered in the unconscious could be related directly to the electrical events neurologists were already familiar with, that the new phenomena would soon be understood in terms of existing physical principles, once a few remaining details were tidied up.

One can hardly quarrel with the idea that brain activity is in some way necessary for mental activity, but the notion that ideas are a kind of fluid stored up in nerve cells, and that chains of associations represent the movement of this fluid along nerve fibers, is a variation on a fantastic theme in nineteenth-century physics. The premature closure with physics that the libido theory represents had an unfortunate impact on Freud's ability to see what was there and no more. It was a retreat from the courageous stance he took in his introduction to "Fragment of an Analysis of a Case of Hysteria" when he indicated without apology that an understanding of neurosis required consideration of "many new things," and that any attempt to reduce them to familiar terms only disguised their true nature.

Later, when the clinical phenomenology of unconscious destructive impulses seemed as out of step with conventional biological thinking as psychic reality had been with physical science, he wrote a book, *Beyond the Pleasure Principle,* in which he attempted to bring about a similarly inappropriate and premature closure between his clinical observations and biological thought. These closures must have relieved some of the strain Freud experienced from dwelling in the continual uncertainty of uncharted psychic reality, without the comfort of any established theoretical underpinning to rest on, and without the examples of forebears to provide encouragement. But they exacted a price in the form of a limitation on the free movement of his mind and his ability to see new things as new.

7

A Specimen Case: Little Hans

F reud's second case history, published a few years after "Fragment of an Analysis of a Case of Hysteria" (known as "Dora"), is titled "Analysis of a Phobia in a Five-Year-Old Boy" (1909), usually known by the pseudonym of its subject, "Little Hans." Of his four case histories, it is the most straightforward and delightful. He intended "Hans" as an illustration of his still-controversial theory of childhood sexuality, which he had put forward four years before, in 1905, just as he had intended "Dora" to be an illustration of his theory linking dreams and neurosis. As was the case with Dora, Freud learned as much from Hans as he taught. Dora's unanticipated lesson had been about the importance of transference in mental life. Hans's was about the nature of anxiety. But although Freud learned the lesson of Dora almost immediately, he was not to appreciate what Hans taught him about anxiety for many years, perhaps because it conflicted at so fundamental a level with his libido theory.

Like Freud's other case histories, "Hans" leaves the reader with the feeling of having known the patient personally, a quality displayed by his clinical writings to a degree unmatched in the psychoanalytic literature. His clinical descriptions are so vivid, astute, and precise that one can deduce from them the operation of finely detailed psychological mechanisms that were unsuspected by him at the time of writing. This case report shows how far his work had progressed in the ten years or so since he first gained insight into the importance of psychic reality in neurosis, and it shows how far he had yet to go in exploiting the opportunity he had created for himself to see things in a new way.

Case History

When Freud undertook his analysis in January 1908, Hans was a little under 5 years old, and had recently experienced the outbreak of a number of severe anxieties: nocturnal fears of losing his mother, fear of going outside, and fear of being bitten by a horse. The analysis began when Hans's father, who had attended a number of Freud's lectures, wrote to him one day that Hans had developed a "nervous disorder."

> One morning, Hans had awakened in tears and had told his mother that when he was asleep he had thought she was gone and he had no Mommy to "coax with" (caress). A few days later he began to cry when taken for walks by his nurse and demanded to be taken back home, although he had been accustomed to taking such walks for quite a while. The following day his mother took him out for a walk, but he was too frightened to go out in the street again and confessed, after some prodding, that he was afraid a horse would bite him.
>
> Freud knew from the father's previous communications that prior to the outbreak of Hans's anxieties, his interest in horses had included a fascination with what he called their "widdlers." Once, seeing a cow being milked, he had exclaimed, "There's milk coming out of its widdler," and he had also watched his mother undress to see if she had one too. He told her that since she was so big, he thought she'd have a widdler like a horse. He had also realized that possession of a widdler had

something to do with being alive. When he had seen water being let out of a steam engine, he said "Oh, look, the engine's widdling. Where's it got its widdler?" but added thoughtfully, "A dog and a horse have widdlers; a table and chair haven't."

Hans's father attempted to dispel his anxieties about being bitten by telling him that Hans was very fond of his mother and had wanted to be taken into her bed (which Hans knew), and that the reason he was so afraid of horses was that he had taken too much interest both in their widdlers and in his own. (This seems to have been an admonition against masturbation, administered on the theory that anxiety was undischarged libido, and that Hans was overaugmenting his by masturbation.) This produced the desired effect of suppressing Hans's worries (or at least his expression of them), but he then contracted influenza and had to stay in bed for two weeks, at the end of which he underwent a tonsillectomy, resulting in a complete relapse of his anxiety symptoms.

At the beginning of March, the family got a new maid with whom Hans was very pleased. She let him ride on her back while she did the cleaning, and he called her "my horse." One day he told her that if she wasn't good, she would have to undress altogether, even taking off her chemise, as a punishment. When the maid did not appear to be properly terrified by this threat, Hans chided her, saying it would be shameful because everyone would "see her widdler." Shortly afterward, he told his father a masturbation fantasy: While he was touching his widdler, he saw his mother naked, showing him her widdler, while he in turn showed his to his friend Grete.

Toward the end of March, on a trip to the zoo, which had formerly been one of Hans's favorite spots, he became frightened for the first time of the large animals, in particular the elephant and the giraffes. There followed a discussion with his father about big animals and their big widdlers, at the conclusion of which Hans said that his widdler would get bigger as he got bigger, reminding himself that "it's fixed in, of course."

A few nights later he became frightened, entered his parent's bedroom, and insisted on getting into bed with them. The next day he told his father the following dream: *In the night there was a big giraffe in the room and a crumpled one; and the big one called out because I took the crumpled one away from it. Then it stopped calling out; and I sat down on top of the crumpled one.* When his father expressed incredulity at the idea of a crumpled giraffe, Hans replied that of course he knew that it was impossible, he had only thought it. The big giraffe had called out, he said, because he had taken the little one away from him. Over the previous few days, Hans had gotten into the habit of coming into his parents' room early in the morning and asking to be taken into their bed. His father would usually protest ("the big one called out because I'd taken the crumpled one away from it"), but his mother finally allowed him into the bed ("Then the big giraffe stopped calling out; and then I sat down on top of the crumpled one.") In Hans's fantasies, the program of activity with his mother had shifted from looking for her widdler to sitting on top of her. Moreover, his dream had provided a link between the feared animals in the zoo and his parents in the bedroom.

Two days following the dream, Hans told his father two dreams or fantasies: In the first, he was crawling under the ropes at the Schoenbrunn Zoo with his father in order to go into a forbidden area that contained some sheep. He had been surprised at how easily he could slip under. He couldn't remember the second thought, but later recalled that it was of smashing a window on a train, in order to gain entry, again accompanied by his father. In both instances a policeman had appeared to apprehend them. Freud commented that this was a most suitable follow-up to the giraffe dream: Hans was aware that possession of his mother was somehow forbidden, but that his father was somehow involved in the forbidden activity. The act itself had now been transformed twice: from looking for his mother's widdler to sitting on her, and from that to entering somewhere forcibly, with a suggestion that the entry was forbidden.

That afternoon, on a visit to Freud, a detail emerged that had not been clear before—namely that Hans was especially bothered by the black area around the horses' mouths. Freud connected this to the father's moustache, and told Hans that it was his father he was afraid of, and precisely because he was so fond of his mother—he feared his father's anger on that account. This produced the first definite improvement in Hans, who was then able to stand in front of his house for a long period of time and watch the horses go by with something approaching equanimity.

The focus of his anxiety now shifted from horses in general to horses hitched to heavily laden carts in particular. He told his father that he was afraid the horse would fall down when the cart turned and "make a row with its feet" as he had seen once when "a horse in a bus" had actually fallen. Hans was afraid that when the horse fell down, it would either die or bite him. At the same time he said that he wished that he could climb up on the horse-drawn carts and load and unload the boxes there, but was also worried that a cart would carry him away. Rather than being alarmed at these apparent complications, Freud noted sanguinely that phobias are in reality multilayered, and that "in consequence of the analysis, not only the patient but the phobia too had plucked up courage and was venturing to show itself."

When his father asked Hans what the horse making a row with its feet reminded him of, he replied that he himself makes a row with his feet when he had to "widdle or make lumf." Shortly afterward, his anxiety became particularly focused on horse-drawn carts that were heavily laden with coal. The row with the feet was thus connected somehow to urination or defecation, and the meaning of the coal was not hard to guess. But beyond this, things were still obscure.

At this point, Hans's mother purchased some new yellow panties for herself, to which he had reacted by spitting and expressing disgust. When his father said he would write about this to Freud, Hans told him to be sure to mention that he'd had the same reaction to her black panties. He then asked his father about ways of avoiding constipation, from which he had suffered in the past. The reaction to the panties was connected to the part of the anatomy they were associated with and to the colors of urine and feces. Despite his disgust at seeing his mother's panties, Hans was also in the habit of pestering his mother to let him watch her "do lumf," an activity that gave him a great deal of pleasure. The disgust and spitting seemed to be a reaction against this pleasure.

In the days following the episode with his mother's panties, Hans began to frisk about, calling himself "a young horse," and when asked if he used to play horses with the children at Gmunden (where the family had summered), he replied, "Yes," and added thoughtfully, "I think that was how I got the nonsense (as he called his phobia)." He then related a story of how a boy named Fritzl, playing a horse, had "run ever so fast," hit his foot on a stone, and fallen down bleeding.

At this point in the report, Freud recalled an earlier episode in Hans's life. When he was 3½ years old, a little more than a year before the onset of his phobia, his mother had given birth to a baby sister. His father had written to Freud on the occasion:

> At five in the morning, labor began and Hans's bed was moved into the next room. He woke up there at seven and, hearing his mother groaning, asked: "Why's Mummy coughing?" Then, after a pause, he said, "The stork's coming today for certain."
>
> Naturally, he has often been told during the last few days that the stork is going to bring a little girl or a little boy; and he quite rightly connected the unusual sounds of groaning with the stork's arrival.
>
> Later on he was taken into the kitchen. He saw the doctor's bag in the front hall and asked: "What's that?" "A bag," was the reply. Upon which he declared with conviction: "The stork's coming to-day." After the baby's delivery the midwife came into the kitchen and Hans heard her ordering some tea to be made. At this he said: "I know! Mummy's to have some tea because she's coughing." He was then called into the bedroom. He did not look at his mother, however, but at the basins and other vessels, filled with blood and water, that were still standing about the room. Pointing to the blood-stained bed-pan, he observed in a surprised voice: "But blood doesn't come out of *my* widdler." [Freud 1909, p. 10]

Freud's narrative now returns to Hans, still telling his father about Gmunden.

> One of the children, Berta, had liked to see him widdle, and he had wanted her to touch his widdler. He then said that "it was such fun at Gmunden. In the little garden where the radishes were there was a little sand-heap; I used to play there with my spade." This was the garden where he used to widdle for Berta.
>
> In mid-April, he told his father that he had "thought of something": He was in a bath, when a plumber came along and unscrewed it to take it away to be repaired. The plumber then took a big borer and stuck it in Hans's stomach. He then allowed that he was afraid of big baths, because he was afraid of being dropped and falling in. There was more about his disgust with lumfs, and he compared horse-drawn carts coming out of gates with lumfs coming out of someone's behind. Having said this, he began referring to such carts as "lumfys," making it sound like a

term of endearment. His aunt's affectionate name for her child was "Wumfy."

Then, in the context of the lumfs and of the fear of falling into the bathwater and disappearing, Hans told his father that he'd thought of his sister Hanna falling off the balcony. This inaugurated a new phase in his analysis in which the theme of Hanna became uppermost. He suggested to his father that they pay the stork not to bring any more babies "out of the big box" where he keeps them. Out on a walk with his father, he tapped the pavement and asked whether people were buried under-neath, or was that just in the cemetery? The question of where people are when they are not on earth (both before and after life) had begun to occupy him. He insisted that Hanna had been with them on a visit to Gmunden they had taken the summer before she was born, in a stork-box in the railway carriage. She had sat in a bath in the box, which was full of babies. The box was painted red (perhaps blood-red, his father thought).

He also told his father that he had wished that Hanna had been let go of when she was having her bath, so she would fall in and die. His father admonished him that a "good boy doesn't wish that sort of thing." "But he may *think* it," said Hans. "But that isn't good," his father replied. To which Hans said, "If he thinks it, it *is* good all the same, because you can write it to the Professor," an observation that prompted Freud to remark that he could wish for no better understanding of psychoanalysis from any grown-up.

Hans then revealed that his fantasy of climbing into the carts and loading and unloading them was connected to another fantasy, that of beating the horses. This made him afraid, as well, because he was afraid he'd actually do it and cause the horses to fall down and "make a row with their feet." When he had seen the bus-horse fall down, he had thought, "Now all the bus horses will have to fall down." He had the beating fantasy "in the morning in bed," he said, and when asked whom he would really like to beat, he had replied, his mother, though he couldn't say why—he would just like to. Hans then explained to his father that buses, furniture vans, and coal carts (all erstwhile objects of fear) were stork-box carts—that is, pregnant women. This suggested to Freud a new meaning for Hans's fears about horses and carts. The horses "making a row with their feet" were connected to his own difficulties passing stool, but also to his mother's having given birth to his sister. The boy playing a horse who had hurt himself and bled was also connected to his father via horses and giraffes, and to the idea of his sister's birth which Hans believed had caused his mother's widdler to bleed. Finally, the rows and pregnancy were also somehow related to his desire to beat his mother.

The following day, Hans had another fright and came running into the house after a coach had passed. He said that the horses were so "proud" (they had been reined in so that their heads were high and their steps short) he was afraid they'd fall down. He said his father was "proud" when he was in bed with his mother, and that he'd wanted his father to fall down like Fritzl, the prancing boy who had cut his foot on a stone. Freud concluded that the desire to beat the horse was compounded from a wish to revenge himself against his father and an obscure sadistic desire for his mother.

The next day, Hans had pushed a small pen-knife through the belly of a rubber doll and tore the doll's legs apart to let the knife fall out. When questioned about it, he said the knife had "belonged to Mommy" and he was getting it for her. This led to a discussion of who has babies, with Hans expressing the opinion that he was going to be the next one in the family to have a baby. When told that he couldn't, he asked if his father could. When told not, he protested that he *belonged* to his father (implying that if his father didn't give birth to him, in what sense could Hans be said to belong to him?). At this point, he was told (somewhat belatedly, considering the perspicacity of his red stork-box fantasy) that babies grow inside their mothers, who bring them into the world by pressing them out like "lumf."

This led to the question of how babies get inside their mothers. Hans had already demonstrated one possible answer by pushing the knife into the doll, and had previously told his father that the stork that brought the babies was the one at the zoo that bit people, which suggested a connection with the fear of biting horses, and also between the stork's knife-shaped beak and the penetrating knife.

Despite his father's caveat, he began to elaborate a fantasy that had occupied him many times before, that of having "his own" children, that is, getting babies from himself. He began to play at loading and unloading cases from a cart, and again referred to the gates of the customs shed opposite his home where the carts exited as "behind-holes."

At the beginning of May, his father asked him if his

"children" were still around, and he replied that they were, but whereas he used to be their mother, he was now their father. A day or two after that, he related a fantasy in which the plumber had reappeared, this time to remove Hans's behind with a pair of pincers, and then do the same with his widdler. He asked to see his father's behind, and his father's widdler, whereupon his father completed the fantasy by saying the plumber had given Hans a bigger behind and a bigger widdler, just like Daddy's. Hans agreed enthusiastically with this. In the course of all of these fantasies coming to light, Hans's fears had largely disappeared.

Freud at the Midpoint of His Development

In his discussion of this report, Freud pointed to the bountiful evidence it contained that sexual interests appear prior to adolescence. The anxieties and symptoms that seemed to be connected to these interests gave him the opportunity to argue the second point he wished to make in publishing the case, that the root of adult neurosis lies in childhood sexual conflicts:

> [When] an adult neurotic patient comes to us for psycho-analytic treatment (and let us assume that his illness has only become manifest after he has reached maturity), we find regularly that his neurosis has as its point of departure an infantile anxiety such as we have been discussing [in the case of Hans] and is in fact a continuation of it; so that, as it were, a continuous and undisturbed thread of psychical activity, taking its start from conflicts of his childhood, has been spun through his life — irrespective of whether the first symptom of those conflicts has persisted or has retreated under the pressure of circumstances. [1909, p. 143]

He added with characteristic boldness that while he was aware that he was "attributing a great deal to the mental capacity of a child between 4 and 5 years of age," he had to let himself be guided "by what we have recently learned [about children's minds], and I do not consider myself to be bound by the prejudices of our ignorance."

At this point in his discussion, Freud had linked together

Hans's fear of horses and of going outside with his fear of his horse-father, with his growing interest in seeing his mother's genitals and in exhibiting his own, with his jealousy of his younger sister, with his hatred of his "proud" father prancing in bed with his mother, and finally with his desire to possess his mother. He had shown with a sure touch how Hans's fantasies about sexual intercourse, pregnancy, and birth had capitalized on bits of external reality such as the horses, carts, crates, zoo animals, buses, and railroad cars as a means of expression.

He continued by turning to the question of why these expressions of unconscious fantasy should be so laden with anxiety — that is, why they constituted a phobia. He suggested at first that, "in our present case of phobia the anxiety is to be explained as being due to the repression of Hans's aggressive propensities (the hostile ones against his father and the sadistic ones against his mother)" (p. 140). But a few pages later he rejected this idea without explanation in favor of one derived from his prepsychoanalytic theory of anxiety neurosis. Hans's anxiety, he says, was the product of a "transformation of libidinal impulses." In support of this, he draws attention to the strength of Hans's attachment to his mother and to his earliest definite symptom: fear at night that his mother had gone and that he had no mother to "coax" with. This, he says, indicates that Hans had strong libidinal impulses toward his mother. His being unable to discharge the built-up libidinal fluid resulted in its stagnation and transformation into anxiety, in the same way that wine turns to vinegar. Hans's libido, Freud goes on to say, had been prevented from discharging itself because he was unable to have sexual intercourse with his mother due to a threat of castration emanating from his father.

But neither the threat nor any indication that Hans's anxiety was transformed libido is presented in the case report. The fluency and openness with which Freud treats the clinical material of Hans's dreams, symptoms, and fantasies is extremely impressive. In comparison, his discussion of the source of Hans's anxiety is strained and contrived, with transformed libido emerging like a deus ex machina.

Freud was indeed "attributing a great deal to the mental capacity of a child of between 4 and 5 years of age," but he erred only in not attributing more, for Hans's view of his world was both more realistic and more fantastic than Freud realized. He underestimated the perceptiveness of Hans's observations of the events in his life, and the rich complexity and subtlety of his fantasies about them, particularly about the birth of his sister and his parents' sexual relationship. Freud also failed to appreciate how profoundly Hands had identified with both parents — by means of his anus, so to speak, with his mother, full of babies and giving birth (his claim that he would be the next to have a baby, his equation of coal with his lumf and coal-carts with pregnant women), and by means of his penis with his father, entering his mother's insides and planting babies there (his activities in the radish garden, his entry into the sheep-pen and the railway-car in the company of his father, his insistence on the red "stork box" that his sister lived in before birth).

These identifications contributed to his anxieties. His desire to load and unload carts, which he equated with his pregnant mother, represents an identification with his father entering his mother to make and deliver babies. The desire is mitigated by his fear that he will be carried off by a cart, which is related to his anxiety that he will fall into the bath and not be able to get out — both expressions of a fear that he will get lost inside his mother during sexual activity.

His identification with his mother was partly — but only partly — in response to this danger, as though he could avoid it by himself becoming a woman, and having his plumber-father insert his borer into Hans's own stomach.

Freud's underestimation of the power of identification is understandable in light of his not yet having had the point brought home to him by clinical experience. He would have this opportunity when he began to explore the problem of melancholia, as outlined in Chapter 8.

A second difficulty in his discussion is more serious and took much longer for him to overcome. When he rejected the idea that Hans's anxieties were related to "repression of his aggressive propensities," and suggested instead that they were due to repression of libidinal urges, Freud was not relying on the clinical evidence represented by Hans's anxieties and fantasies. Rather, Freud was trying to mold the evidence to conform to his physical model, which held that anxiety is the product of repressed sexual excitation accumulating as undischarged "sub-cortical excitation," or, in the

more picturesque expression he sometimes used, "fermented libido."
The difficulty with this is seen more easily if the quasiphysical
terminology is translated into ordinary English: Hans's desire to
have sexual intercourse with his mother, when frustrated, gives rise
not to disappointment or sadness, but automatically and inevitably
to anxiety. Why this should occasion so much anxiety in him, when
none of the vital aspects of his relationship to his mother is in
jeopardy, and when a 5-year-old boy is incapable of sexual intercourse in any event, is not at all clear.

It is here that the trajectory of Freud's explorations as a
psychological phenomenologist who uses his "organ for the perception of psychical qualities" to establish contact with Hans is inter-
cepted by his preoccupation with tying his observations to solid
physical ground. But the phenomenologist eventually prevailed: In
time, Freud allowed himself to be led by the clinical evidence into
abandoning the libido theory of anxiety. This development, and the
reasons for it, will be described in Chapters 9 and 10.

8

Identification and the
Structure of the Inner World

F reud recognized the rich potential of unconscious identification for building a complex, dynamic inner world with a life of its own several years after his analysis of Hans, through his attempts to treat patients with severe depression. For many years this disorder had defied psychoanalytic treatment. The reasons for this were partly technical: Patients who are severely depressed are also quite withdrawn and are therefore little able to cooperate in the treatment, but the lack of success in treating such patients was mainly due to a lack of theoretical knowledge about how such states of mind arose. As late as 1910, Freud had declared the psychological problem of melancholia, as it was then called, to be insoluble.

Then, in 1911, Karl Abraham, a student and colleague of Freud's, published a paper describing his work, "Notes on the Psychoanalytical Investigation and Treatment of Manic-Depressive Insanity and Allied Conditions," in which he pointed out the similarities between severe depression and the normal process of mourning. He also reported making substantial headway in the treatment of a case of manic-depressive psychosis by psychoanalysis.

Identification

A few years later, Freud published his landmark paper "Mourning and Melancholia" (1917), in which he recognized for the first time the immense importance of identification in the genesis of melancholia, and gave it a new and profound psychoanalytic meaning. He begins with a comparison of mourning and melancholia, noting that both are accompanied by a "profoundly painful dejection, cessation of interest in the outside world, loss of the capacity to love and inhibition of all activity." He continues by observing that

> in mourning we find that the inhibition and loss of interest are fully accounted for by the work of mourning in which the ego [the self] is absorbed. . . . The inhibition of the melancholic seems puzzling because we cannot see what is absorbing him so entirely. The melancholic displays something else which is lacking in mourning—an extraordinary diminution in his self-regard, an impoverishment of his ego on a grand scale. In mourning, it is the world which has become poor and empty; in melancholia it is the ego itself. The patient represents his ego to us as worthless, incapable of any achievement and morally despicable; he reproaches himself, vilifies himself and expects to be cast out and punished. He abases himself before everyone and commiserates with his own relatives for being connected with anyone so unworthy. He is not of the opinion that a change has taken place in him, but extends his self-criticism back over the past; he declares that he was never any better. This picture of a delusion of (mainly moral) inferiority is completed by sleeplessness and refusal to take nourishment, and—what is psychologically very remarkable—by an overcoming of the instinct which compels every living thing to cling to life. . . .
>
> [But] it must strike us that after all the melancholic does not behave in quite the same way as a person who is crushed by remorse and self-reproach in a normal fashion. Feelings of shame in front of other people, which would more than anything

characterize this latter condition, are lacking in the melancholic, or at least they are not very prominent in him. One might emphasize the presence in him of an almost opposite trait of insistent communicativeness which finds satisfaction in self-exposure. . . .

There is one observation, not at all difficult to make, which leads to the explanation of the contradiction. . . . If one listens patiently to a melancholic's many and various self-accusations, one cannot in the end avoid the impression that often the most violent of them are hardly at all applicable to the patient himself, but that with insignificant modifications they do fit someone else, someone the patient loves or has loved or should love. Each time one examines the facts this conjecture is confirmed. So we find the key to the clinical picture: we perceive that the self-reproaches are reproaches against a loved object which has been shifted away from it on to the patient's own ego. . . .

Their complaints are really "plaints" in the old sense of the word. They are not ashamed and do not hide themselves, since everything derogatory they say about themselves is at bottom said about someone else. Moreover, they are far from evincing towards those around them the attitude of humility and submissiveness that would alone befit such worthless people. On the contrary, they make the greatest nuisance of themselves, and always seem as though they felt slighted and had been treated with great injustice. All this is possible only because the reactions expressed in their behavior still proceed from a mental constellation of revolt, which has then, by a certain process, passed over into the crushed state of melancholia. [1917, pp. 245–248]

The process by which a state of revolt passes over to a crushed state in melancholia is identification, as a result of which the ego of the subject becomes somehow equated with the person against whom a grievance is held, or as Freud more succinctly puts it, "the shadow of the object falls upon the ego."[1]

-----

[1]Since the term *object* is apt to be misleading in this context, a brief digression through its usage in psychoanalysis might be in order. Recall that when Freud formulated his theory of sexuality, he established the convention of referring to the target of an instinctual impulse as the object of that impulse. In common usage, of

Freud believed that identification itself operates only by virtue of an instinctual drive: The melancholic has "regressed," as he puts it, to the earliest, oral stage of sexual development, and his ego "wants to incorporate the object into itself and, in accordance with the oral or cannibalistic phase of libidinal development in which it is, wants to do so by devouring it."

In other words, identification is the result of the ego having devoured an object in fantasy. But this is a fantasy with a very real (subjective) effect: It leads to a real alteration of the psychological state of things. We note that Freud considered that the fantasy capable of accomplishing such an effect must be an expression of an instinctual force, like the unconscious fantasies that instigate dreams.

Although Freud characterized the instinctual force that operates in the process of identification as "oral libido," the way in which he now used the term shows that he had in mind something quite different from the fluid of the old physical model. There, the aim of an instinct was to bring about discharge of libido, a lowering of tension in the system as a whole. In identification, an instinctual drive — orality — accomplishes not a discharge of tension but something quite different: a building-up or alteration of the structure of the mind by a process of incorporating something from the outside world into it.

The physical basis of a process such as identification is very difficult to visualize in terms of the ebb and flow of libido, and here Freud does not even attempt to suggest what it might be. He now seems content to let his clinical perceptions outreach the tether of his physical theories.

The melancholic patient, then, has an instinctually driven fantasy of devouring the object, as a result of which he comes to feel that he has concretely taken it inside himself, and that the object exists not only in the external world but also in an internal one. This

---

course, "object" normally refers specifically to something *non*human, whereas in psychoanalysis it refers to something specifically *human:* a person, or a part of a person, or something that represents one of these in the unconscious. It is an unfortunate linguistic turn of events, and the potential for confusion among those unfamiliar with its technical meaning is obvious.

means that he has come to experience himself in some way *as* the object. The melancholic withdraws his interest from the outside world because he is preoccupied with the "world" inside himself, created by identification.

The inner world so created is experienced unconsciously as literally populated by those with whom we have identified ourselves via the ties of love or hate. Although to an observer the mental mechanism of identification might be an unconscious fantasy, to the subject it is a straightforward fact of his subjective existence.

The Structure of the Inner World

In "Mourning and Melancholia" Freud describes for the first time in detail how an unconscious fantasy, linked to an instinctual force, could alter the structure of the mind itself. In the years that followed, he went on to delineate the role of identification in the normal building up of the mind's structure as well:

> [In "Mourning and Melancholia"] we succeeded in explaining the painful disorder of melancholia by supposing that [in those suffering from it] an object which was lost had been set up inside the ego. . . . At that time, however, we did not appreciate *how common and how typical* it is. Since then we have come to understand how this kind of substitution has a great share in determining the form taken by the ego and that it makes an essential contribution towards building up what is called its "character." . . . When it happens that a person has to give up [any] object, there quite often ensues an alteration of his ego which can only be described as a setting up of the object within his ego, as it occurs in melancholia. . . . It may be that this introjection . . . makes it easier for the object to be given up or renders that process possible. . . . At any rate the process, especially in the early phases of development, is a very frequent one, and it makes it possible to suppose that the character of the ego is a precipitate of abandoned object[s] . . . and that it contains a history of [its] object-choices. [emphasis mine] [1923, pp. 28–29]

Identification is of particular importance early in life, since it

is known to psychoanalysis as the earliest expression of an
emotional tie with another person. It plays a part in the early
history of the Oedipus complex. A little boy will exhibit a special
interest in his father; he would like to grow like him and be like
him, and take his place everywhere. We may simply say that he
takes his father as his ideal. This behavior has nothing to do with
a passive or feminine attitude toward his father (and towards
males in general); it is on the contrary typically masculine. It fits
in well with the Oedipus complex, for which it helps to prepare
the way. [1921, p. 105]

In Freud's view, identification not only sets the stage for the
Oedipus complex, it also brings about its resolution. When the child
is placed in a position of rivalry with one parent, whom the child also
loves, for the possession of the other parent, any outcome would lead
to an extremely painful loss. The dilemma is resolved by the child's
identifying with the parents. By becoming like the father through
identification, the child can allow him to have certain exclusive
prerogatives with the mother without suffering unbearable envy and
jealousy; likewise, by becoming like the mother through identification, the child can allow her certain prerogatives with the father.
These two identifications together then constitute a permanent
"agency" within the mind that acts as a kind of internal parent,
distinct from the ego and experienced as somehow above it: the
superego.

Although both the ego and the superego are parts of the inner
world, the superego is experienced as distinct from ourselves,
whereas the ego forms the core of our psychological being. Freud
eventually delineated two kinds of identification. The first, the type
we have just discussed, aids in the child's resolution of the Oedipus
complex, and contributes to the formation of the superego. A second
type, beginning earlier in life, contributes to the building up of the
ego, or sense of self.

Armed with a model within which he could conceive of the
complexities of one's relationship with oneself, Freud could now
return to deal in a more sophisticated way with the problem of
neurotic anxiety that had given him such difficulty with Hans.

9

Anxiety and the Structure of the Inner World

More than 15 years after he had formulated his explanation of Hans's anxieties in terms of the "fermentation" of repressed libido, Freud returned again to the problem of the origin of neurotic anxiety, and in 1926 published a book, *Inhibitions, Symptoms and Anxiety* (1926), devoted to answering, or at least clarifying, this question.

What strikes one first about the book is the absence of the methodical, fluid line of argument typical of Freud's work. As a rule, his writing conveys the impression that he is whittling away at a problem even as he writes about it. The argument is pursued confidently: A problem is posed, the possible solutions outlined, each considered in turn and weighed on its merits, objections to proposed solutions are dealt with, an appeal to clinical experience is made at a crucial juncture, a solution is adopted, and finally, perhaps some newly revealed connections between the original problem and related problems are indicated, serving as an agenda for future research.

This familiar pattern is barely present in *Inhibitions, Symptoms and Anxiety.* Rather than proceeding in his usual methodical way, he treats the same subject in similar terms at different places. He needs three addenda to tidy up the issues raised in ten chapters, and he seesaws a great deal between alternative points of view whose relationships to one another are never clarified. The lack of unity is both uncharacteristic and striking. One has the impression that he is trying to struggle his way out of a problem into which he keeps falling back, as though something had dulled his usually sure, incisive intelligence.

Abandoning the Libido Theory of Anxiety

At the age of nearly 70, Freud had to face the fact that his libido theory of anxiety, an important part of the physical model to which he still half hoped to return, was no longer secure. The painful conflict this caused him is especially evident in the circuitousness of the part of the book containing his critical reexamination of the analysis of Hans, in which he reviews his libido theory of anxiety in the light of 25 years of phenomenological observation, and decides finally and with palpable regret to replace it with a psychological theory.

He begins *Inhibitions, Symptoms and Anxiety* by

> reviewing the little boy's psychical situation as a whole as it came to light in the course of the analytic treatment. He was at the time in the jealous and hostile Oedipus attitude toward his father, whom nevertheless — except in so far as his mother was the cause of the estrangement — he dearly loved. Here, then, we have a conflict due to ambivalence: a well-grounded love and a no less justifiable hatred directed toward one and the same person. "Little Hans's" phobia must have been an attempt to solve this conflict [by repression]. . . . The instinctual impulse which underwent repression in "Little Hans" was a hostile one against his father. [1926, p. 101]

He then asks us to set aside the factors of Hans's mixed feelings about his father and his tender age and imagine an analogous situation in which "a young servant is in love with the mistress of the house and has received some tokens of her favour. He hates his master, who is more powerful than he is, and would like to have him out of the way" (pp. 102–103). It would then be eminently natural, Freud reasons, for the servant to dread his master's vengeance and to develop a fear of him. What made Hans's emotional reaction a neurosis seemed to be only one thing: the replacement of his father by a horse. However, this formulation poses another problem that he immediately recognizes:

> It would have been more in accordance with our expectations if "Little Hans" had developed, instead of a fear of horses, an inclination to ill-treat them and beat them or if he had expressed in plain terms a wish to see them fall down or be hurt or even die in convulsions ("make a row with their feet"). Something of this sort did in fact emerge in his analysis, but it was not by any means in the forefront of his neurosis. And, curiously enough, if he really had produced a hostility of this sort not against his father but against horses as his main symptom, we should not have said he was suffering from a neurosis. There must be something wrong either with our view of repression or with our definition of a symptom. [1926, p. 103]

This impasse was a source of frustration and disappointment to Freud:

> It is almost humiliating that, after working so long, we should still be having difficulty in understanding the most fundamental facts. . . . But we have made up our minds to simplify nothing and to hide nothing. If we cannot see things clearly we will at least see clearly what the obscurities are. [1926, p. 124]

A Psychological Theory of Anxiety

The theory that neurotic symptoms and anxiety are due to repressed erotic impulses, when examined closely in the light of clinical evidence, turned out to lead to unforeseen complexities and dead ends. Freud then makes explicit a point that he had already put forward in "Hans," but had not hitherto tied directly to anxiety or symptoms:

> It seems to me that . . . we can detect [that] the motive force of the repression was . . . the fear of impending castration. "Little Hans" gave up his aggressiveness toward his father from a fear of being castrated. His fear that a horse would bite him can, without any forcing, be given the full sense of a fear that a horse would bite off his genitals, would castrate him.
>
> Here, then, is our unexpected finding. . . . The idea contained in [the] anxiety—being bitten by a horse [was a] substitute by distortion for the idea of being castrated by [the] father. . . . *It was anxiety which produced repression and not, as I formerly believed, repression which produced anxiety* [emphasis added]. . . .
>
> It is no use denying the fact, though it is not pleasant to recall it, that I have on many occasions asserted that in repression the instinctual representative [the idea associated with an instinctual impulse] is distorted, displaced, and so on, while the libido belonging to the instinctual impulse is transformed into anxiety. But now an examination of phobias, which should be best able to provide confirmatory evidence, fails to bear out my assertion; it seems, rather, to contradict it directly. [1926, pp. 108–109]

After struggling through his critique of libido theory, he was forced to conclude that neither anxiety nor neurotic symptoms were progeny of repressed libido. Instead, neurotic symptoms seemed to arise as defenses against anxiety. Neurotic anxiety itself arose in turn—if not from repressed libido, then from what? Freud was again faced with the problem he had failed to deal with adequately at the time of "Hans," the causes of neurotic anxiety.

His closer examination of the phobic symptoms had shown that they evolved in connection with an anxiety about being mutilated. Freud describes this as "a realistic fear, a fear of a danger which was actually impending or was judged to be a real one" (p. 108).

The description of the fear of castration as realistic gives rise to evident ambiguities. It is unlikely that Freud considered the danger of either of his patients' castration by their fathers to be a real one, and it is hard to believe that he had lost his normally critical attitude toward a danger "judged to be a real one." He had too much experience with the unreliability of human judgment to commit that sort of error. He meant that the anxiety was about a danger that was real in the child's internal world.

The cause of the repression of Hans's genital impulses for his mother now receives a new answer. It was an attempt to render manageable a severe, terrifying internal anxiety. His neurotic symptoms were defenses against an anxiety arising in the internal world, and the form of each symptom was dictated by the nature of the anxiety and of the defenses against it. The reappraisal undertaken in *Inhibitions, Symptoms and Anxiety* had strengthened Freud's belief in his psychological theory of neurosis — that is, his estimation of the importance to neurosis of events occurring in the internal world. At the same time, the role of a physical entity such as libido in the production of anxiety, the question of "the material out of which anxiety is made," as Freud put it, now "loses its interest" (1933, p. 85).

The repression of the sexual impulses associated with the Oedipus period was due to anxiety, and this anxiety was due in turn to a "real" threat of castration — one that had psychic reality. How had the threat become established in the internal world? Nearly 20 years after he had unified neurotic symptoms, slips, dreams, and transference under the aegis of his "psychological theory," Freud now approached the problem of neurotic anxiety from the same point of view: It is due to the presence of a figure in the internal world that threatens castration and that in turn arises like a dream, the result of a melding together of the perception of external realities with unconscious impulses and fantasies.

In arguing this, Freud pointed out that any child would certainly have external perceptions of loss on which to rely for a model for castration: weaning, which had meant a loss of the breast, and elimination, which, during the anal period when feces are highly valued, is also experienced as a loss. He even considered the possibility that birth itself, with its loss of the comforts of the womb, was the prototype of all such losses. Such material losses, he reasoned, would produce anxiety about an immaterial one: the loss of the parents' love. This in turn would pass over into an anxiety about the loss of love from the *internalized* parents, the superego. The force behind neurosis was an anxiety stemming from an internal threat to a relationship within the mind, between the ego and the superego.

But he goes on to point out that it was also clear that other factors must be operating as well. In the first place, the normal emotional reaction to separation or loss of love is pain and mourning, not anxiety. Of equal importance, there were cases in which the severity of the superego exceeded the harshness with which the child had been treated by the actual parents. Since the superego is formed by identification with the parents, Freud argues, we are forced to the conclusion that something happens to the neurotic-to-be's experience of the actual parents during the process of identification to distort it in the direction of harshness.

The additional factor is the child's own aggressive impulses toward the parents, which mix in with perceptions of the actual parents in the process of identification to produce the superego. In a lecture series he wrote in 1933, Freud offers the following account of his new theory:

> The super-ego . . . takes over the power, function and even the methods of the parental agency . . . [but there is] a discrepancy between the two. [In neurosis] the super-ego seems to have made a one-sided choice and to have picked out only the parent's strictness and severity, their prohibiting and punitive function, whereas their loving care seems not to have been taken over and maintained. If the parents have really enforced their authority with severity we can easily understand the child's in turn developing a severe super-ego. But, contrary to our expectation, experience shows that the super-ego can acquire the same characteristic of relentless severity even if the upbringing had been mild and kindly and had so far as possible avoided threats and punishments. . . . There is no doubt that, when the super-ego was first instituted, in equipping that agency use was made of a piece of the child's aggressiveness towards his parents . . . and for that reason the severity of the super-ego need not simply correspond to the strictness of the upbringing. [p. 62]

A few years before, he put the same point this way:

Experience shows . . . that the severity of the super-ego which a child develops in no way corresponds to the severity of treatment which he has himself met with (as has rightly been emphasized by Melanie Klein and other English writers). The severity of the former seems to be independent of that of the latter. A child who has been very leniently brought up can acquire a very strict conscience. But it would also be wrong to exaggerate this independence; it is not difficult to convince oneself that severity of upbringing does also exert a strong influence on the formation of the child's super-ego. What it amounts to is that in the formation of the super-ego and the emergence of a conscience innate constitutional factors and influences from the real environment act in combination. This is not at all surprising; on the contrary, it is a universal aetiological condition for all such processes. [1930, p. 130]

This "universal etiological condition for all such processes" is the one we are familiar with from the process of dreaming. With this phrase, Freud includes identification, and its most important product, the superego, in the group of phenomena obeying the psychological law of the "etiologic series," the blending of external and internal realities. Hans's castration anxiety was a fear of his superego and was an alloy of external and internal factors because its source was itself such an alloy.

This composite nature of the superego is indicated by a dream reported by a patient in analysis:

The patient had parked his car while shopping at a supermarket and returned to it to find a dent in the driver's door. He noticed that another car, which he recognized as the analyst's, was parked alongside his, and that one of its side mirrors had been damaged. When he looked back at his own car, he saw a fragment of mirror embedded in the dent, and as he stared at it, saw an eye looking back at him. It took him a moment to realize it was the reflection of his own eye.

The mirror embedded in the patient's car represented his superego, a parent (represented by the analyst) who had become embedded in the patient's mind, acting as an observer inside the patient. This is the parent's contribution to the superego. But the eye that watches from the mirror is the patient's own, indicating that his superego's way of looking at him contains an element of his own way of looking at others. This is the patient's contribution to his superego. The two contributions combine to form a superego embedded in the patient whose scrutiny of him is the product not only of the mirror-parents, but also of a part of the patient — his "eye" or way of looking at things — that had itself become embedded in the parents.

Unconscious castration anxiety, which Freud had implicated as the cause of repression in Hans, turned out not to be the sole type of neurotic anxiety but only one of a large class of anxieties, all manifestations of persecution arising from a harsh superego formed in the manner Freud had outlined. The way in which the child comes to experience his own aggressiveness as the parent's (and later the superego's) aggressiveness toward him is a complex process, the precise development of which was later elucidated by Klein.

A careful scrutiny of one of the simplest of neurotic symptoms, a childhood phobia, led to the unexpected result that repression was not the cause of anxiety, as the libido theory of anxiety posited, but was its result. The focus of the attempt to unravel the nature of neurosis now had to be shifted to the roots of neurotic anxiety, which seemed to reside in the relationship between the ego and the superego. Because of the manner in which the superego is formed, this relationship is connected both to the actual relationship between child and parents and to the child's aggressiveness toward the parents, which colors the eventual character of the superego and makes it, in neurotic states, harsher and more aggressive than the actual parents were. Because of this compound, dreamlike origin, the superego becomes a source of the severest and most fantastic anxieties. The apparently simple finding that anxiety is prior to repression set in motion the last important development in Freud's thinking, his theory of infantile aggression.

10

Beyond Eros

F reud's realization that a child's sexual impulses produce a concrete fantasy — a subjectively real, dreamlike unconscious experience — of the parents imposing themselves on the child sexually, was the first of a series of discoveries that he summarized by saying that in neurosis, psychic reality was of greater importance than material reality. The discovery of infantile sexuality led him to the theory of the Oedipus complex as well as to the psychoanalytic treatment of neurosis.

After his reappraisal of the nature of neurotic anxiety in *Inhibitions, Symptoms and Anxiety,* which showed that it was not a physiologic intoxication with undischarged libido but the consequence of a relationship between the ego and the superego, he was now in a position to make another discovery quite similar to, and quite as important as, the earlier one about unconscious incestuous fantasies.

A terrifying or anxiety-provoking superego may be thought of as a concrete fantasy—a subjectively real, dreamlike unconscious experience—of an internal parent imposing itself on one aggressively. Freud reasoned that if the theory of the Oedipus complex is correct—that is, if the child's Oedipal fantasies of a molesting parent are products of the child's sexual impulses—then a fantastically terrifying internal parent must in some way represent the child's aggressive impulses.

The Destructive Instinct

Freud usually referred to aggressive impulses as the products of an "aggressive drive." But at other times he called it a "destructive drive," an ambiguity in terminology that reflects an ambivalence in his thinking. The term *aggressive* is more equivocal than the term *destructive*. Infantile aggression can be subsumed under the already accepted instincts of sexuality or self-preservation, as a subsidiary acting in their service. This is in fact how many analysts now view it. But if this were all Freud meant by it, he would not have found it necessary to postulate a new drive; he could have simply spoken of the vigor of the old drives, or of the vigor with which one pursues one's sexual or self-preservative goals, which is usually referred to as "healthy aggression." But this is precisely what he did *not* mean: He postulated a separate drive because he was trying to frame in words something else, a force that is fundamentally antisexual and antiself-preservative, destructive of that on which life depends, and ultimately of life itself. Only something along the line of a destructive drive would correspond to the apparently senseless devastation inflicted on the psyche by the neurotic superego whose nature he was trying to fathom.

The strongest line of clinical evidence for such a drive was provided by the phenomenon of "moral masochism," a form of neurotic suffering in which

the suffering itself is what matters; whether it is decreed by someone who is loved or someone who is indifferent is of no importance. It may even be caused by impersonal powers or circumstances; the true masochist always turns his cheek whenever he has a chance of receiving a blow. [1924, p. 165]

Moral masochism enters the psychoanalytic setting in a specifically psychoanalytic manifestation, the negative therapeutic reaction (Freud 1916). This is the alarming tendency of certain patients to react to well-timed, well-phrased, substantially correct interpretations, the mother's milk of psychoanalysis, as though they had been given psychological poison. The analyst's initial assumption when the patient worsens in response to an interpretation is that it must have been incorrect. Since it is impossible to establish beyond all doubt that an interpetation is correct, this assumption must be made in every such case. But long experience gave rise to the suspicion, which grew in time to a conviction, that certain patients *characteristically* react badly to interpretations that are, as the patients themselves recognize later, both correct and well timed.

Further, attempts to treat the negative therapeutic reaction as ordinary resistance by attempting to interpret the anxiety underlying it seems only to make it worse, and only the analyst's leading the analysis further and further away from the gist of the patient's unconscious mental life seems to quell it.

Freud recognized that this untoward reaction to an interpretation occurred precisely *because* the analysis was proceeding along correct lines. This reaction, he said,

> constitutes . . . the greatest danger to the success of our medical or educative aims. . . . It is instructive, too, to find, contrary to all theory and expectation, that a neurosis which has defied every therapeutic effort may vanish if the subject becomes involved in the misery of an unhappy marriage, or loses all his money, or develops a dangerous organic disease. In such instances one form of suffering has been replaced by another; and we see that all that mattered was that it should be possible to maintain a certain amount of suffering. [1924, p. 166]

These patients, who react badly to helpful interpretations, react well when they have been harmed by something. Freud concluded that this perverse combination of distress and satisfaction indicated that the superego, for some reason, had become destructive of the self: "harsh, cruel and inexorable against the ego which is in its charge."

The existence of an internal parent that threatens castration when no such threat had been made in external reality, and the moral masochist's being "harmed" by good fortune and "healed" by bad, constituted Freud's two main lines of evidence for postulating a destructive instinct. Such an instinct feeds into the child's experiences of external reality to produce a murderous superego "parent" in the same way that the child's erotic instincts melded with experiences to produce the sexually seductive parent of oedipal psychic reality. The more Freud thought about the ramifications of this idea, the more important it seemed to him, and in a paper published the year before he died (1937), he wondered whether "all we know about psychical conflict should not be revised from this new angle" of the struggle between the sexual and the destructive instincts.

The idea of an innate destructive force remains, even today, the most controversial of Freud's theories. If not the newest of the "many new things" he had seen through his psychoanalytic approach, it is certainly the hardest to swallow. Many analysts simply ignore it, and speak as though Freud had merely been describing healthy aggression. Freud himself left the door open to this dismissal of his finding by the ambiguity of the language he used to describe it, which, like the earlier ambivalent use of the term *libido,* allowed him to write in a way that made it perfectly unclear at times whether he was describing something familiar like healthy aggression, or something very new and, to conventional ways of thinking, very bizarre.

He tried at first to make the strangeness of the notion of a destructive instinct familiar in much the same way as he had earlier introduced the notion of libido as a physical substance to make his theory of neurosis seem more grounded in the "real" world of physiology. He argued in *Beyond the Pleasure Principle* (1920) that a destructive drive was no more than a manifestation of a general biological phenomenon, pointing to biological evidence of a substance that accumulated in all cells and tissues, and that led inevitably to their death. But he did not place as much emphasis on these biological speculations as he had on his theory of libido, being able to recognize at this stage of his career that a destructive instinct manifesting itself as a psychological phenomenon must stand or fall on psychoanalytic evidence alone; or rather, that clinical psychoanalytic observation had sufficient dignity to serve as the basis of his hypotheses about instincts without needing to be shored up with observations from other fields.

With this, he could drop his semiapologetic attempt to make the strangeness of his findings seem familiar, and go on, this time rather defiantly, to wonder only what had prevented him from seeing them sooner. He recognized that the notion of a destructive instinct "is felt by many people as an innovation and, indeed, as a most undesirable one which should be gotten rid of as quickly as possible" (1933, p. 103). But he detected a

> strong affective factor . . . coming into effect in this rejection. Why have we ourselves needed such a long time before we decided to recognize an aggressive instinct? . . . We should probably have met with little resistance if we had wanted to ascribe an instinct with such an aim to animals. But to include it in the human constitution appears sacrilegious; it contradicts too many religious presumptions and social conventions. No, man must be naturally good or at least good-natured. If he occasionally shows himself brutal, violent or cruel, these are only passing disturbances of his emotional life, for the most part provoked, or perhaps only the consequences of the inexpedient social regulations which he has hitherto imposed on himself. [1933, p. 103]

It seems unlikely that he is writing here of healthy aggression.

The destructive instinct, notwithstanding Freud's temporary attempts to biologize it, is a distinctive *psychoanalytic* observation arrived at by means of psychoanalytic contact with patients. There is nothing in physics or biology that is precisely analogous to it. Whatever its validity or usefulness, this is of real significance: That Freud was able to postulate such a fundamentally psychological force solely on the basis of *clinical* evidence was a triumph of his conviction about the reality of psychological realities and of the power of the psychoanalytic approach to reveal them.

His method had first allowed him to see how dreams were formed by the melding of external events with wishes, desires, and impulses arising from within. He then saw how dreaming was in this respect only one of a family of psychological phenomena obeying this dialectical formula he called an "etiological series," which included neurotic symptoms, unintentional slips, transference, identification, and finally, the structure of the mind itself. He used each member of this family, as it was discovered, as a conceptual tool for discovering others. Dreaming led to his understanding of the emotional dynamism of neurosis; his understanding of neurosis allowed him to detect transference; transference, he saw, was based on internal figures formed by identifications and exchangeable in a sense with outer ones; and the phenomenon of identification, with its interchange between the inner and outer worlds, enabled him to see how the very structure of the mind arose. Now past 80, he had created, nurtured, and defended—against himself as well as others—a new and systematic way of investigating the mind. The burden of further development now fell on others who could take these findings as a given.

PART II

Melanie Klein's Development of Freud's Work

11

Melanie Klein's Place in Psychoanalysis

At the heart of Freud's thinking about the mind is a to-and-fro dialectic between fantasy and external reality: A piece of external reality is melded with an unconscious fantasy to form a psychic reality. The unconscious fantasy must be "wishful" in nature, which means that it must be a derivative, near or distant, of an instinctual impulse. This dialectic produces an internal reality, which then has a life and psychological meaning of its own. On this basis he understood first the phenomenon of dreaming, and then the formation of neurotic symptoms, transference, identification, the building-up of mental structures such as the superego, and finally, the roots of neurotic anxiety. It was not external events themselves that operated the wheels of the mind, but the specific, idiosyncratic, unconscious *meaning* of events, that melding of internal factors with external reality that constitutes psychic reality.

Among those who took this psychological perspective as a given, the British psychoanalyst Melanie Klein stands preeminent.

Her thinking, free of the physical preoccupations against which Freud had to struggle, is concerned only with the many ramifications of the *psychological* phenomena that he discovered. Her work rests on the exploration of psychic realities that lay at the heart of Freud's psychological approach to the mind. It illuminates and exemplifies, in an unprecedentedly clear and straightforward way, what is distinctive in psychoanalysis.

Klein was born in Vienna in 1882, a generation later than Freud. She began her psychoanalytic work in Berlin in 1919, and by 1925 she had become preeminent in the field of the psychoanalysis of children. She was invited to London from Berlin by Ernest Jones, the biographer of Freud and the founder and president of the British Psycho-Analytical Society, to give a series of lectures to the society based on her work. She traveled again to London the following year under Jones's patronage and remained there to work, train other analysts, teach, and write until her death in 1960.

In an introduction to a collection of her papers, Jones (1948) places her work in the overall context of the development of psychoanalytic thought:

> Freud's investigation of the unconscious mind, which is essentially that of the young infant, had revealed unexpected aspects of childhood, but before Mrs. Klein there had been little attempt to confirm these discoveries by the direct study of childhood. To her, therefore, is due the credit of carrying psycho-analysis to where it principally belongs—the heart of the child. . . . She developed fearlessly the play-technique of interpretation, using it in combination with various other activities and was soon in a position to confirm at first hand all that Freud had inferred from adult material concerning the hitherto unknown unconscious mind of the child. Encouraged by this she exploited to the full the favorable opportunity she had created for herself and determined to pursue her investigations to their uttermost limit. . . .
>
> Mrs. Klein's boldness did not stop at the study of normal and neurotic infantile development. She has extended it into the field of insanity itself . . . But the extension was inescapable. The resemblance between certain infantile processes and those so blatant in paranoia, schizophrenia and manic-depressive insanity could not be overlooked by someone of Mrs. Klein's

perspicacity . . . I am confident that Mrs. Klein's work will prove as fruitful in this field as it has already shown itself to be in the more familiar one of neurotic and normal development. [1948, pp. 338–339]

Klein's method for direct observation of the unconscious mind of the child sprang from her appreciation of the fact (which Freud learned from Hans) that children's spontaneous play was a form of communication about their unconscious, equal in precision and eloquence to the free associations of adults. This meant that one could establish direct psychoanalytic contact with the mind of a child by observing the child's play. Klein devised a psychoanalytic technique based on this finding, by means of which she could psychoanalyze children as young as two and three-quarter years, too young to communicate freely in any other way about their internal states. She discovered that even these small children form transferences to the analyst that, like those of adults, offer an unparalleled opportunity to observe states of mind that existed even earlier in their lives. She was now in a position not only to observe directly those features of children's mental life that Freud had only been able to reconstruct from his analyses of adults, but also to detect for the first time the psychological events that dominate the minds of infants and form the developmental basis for the psychology of childhood that Freud delineated:

> The play technique . . . allowed me to draw new conclusions about the very early stages of infancy and deeper layers of the unconscious. Such retrospective insight is based on the crucial finding of Freud, the transference situation, that is to say the fact that in a psychoanalysis the patient re-enacts in relation to the psychoanalyst earlier—and, I would add, even very early— situations and emotions. . . . It is part of the technique of the psychoanalyst to deduce the past from these manifestations. . . .
> Since I had the good fortune to analyze very young children, I was able to gain an . . . insight into their mental life, which led back to an understanding of the mental life of the baby. For I was enabled by the meticulous attention I paid to the transference in the play technique to come to a deeper understanding of the ways in which—in the child and later also in the adult—

mental life is influenced by the earliest emotions and unconscious phantasies. . . . [1959, p. 245]

To Klein's mind, the psychoanalysis of children was an inevitable
extension of Freud's work: She took quite literally the notion that, in
establishing contact with the unconscious of an adult, psychoanalysis was speaking to a child, and she regarded psychoanalysis as an
unquestionably natural means of communication with children. As
Freud's analyses had revealed the child within every adult, Klein's
explorations revealed the baby inside that child. Her way of thinking
was, as Jones put it, "very alien to those who accept [Freud's]
findings . . . providing they are not taken too seriously" (Jones
1952, p. 341).

Klein's focus on the unconscious of the child gave her a great
appreciation and respect for the power of psychic reality in the
workings of the mind. The unconscious of the child, like the deepest
and most fundamental layers of the adult's unconscious with which
it is synonymous, is virtually dominated by psychic reality; its
contents and mode of operation are highly fantastic and quite
removed from the ways of external reality.

After developing her technique for psychoanalyzing children,
she made a series of advances that were so dramatic and rapid that
Freud himself was left somewhat stunned and disbelieving. A
number of letters between Freud and Jones have recently been
published (Steiner 1985) that reveal his early skepticism about
Klein's ideas. The situation was complicated somewhat by the fact
that, by the late 1920s, Freud's daughter Anna, who had also
recently begun work in child analysis, had stated her firm opposition
to a number of Klein's views on child analysis. It is difficult to know
how much of Freud's reaction to Klein was connected to a father's
desire to take Anna's side, but it is unlikely that he was motivated
entirely by paternal loyalty.

Freud's Comments on Klein

The correspondence begins with Jones writing to Freud in June
1925 that Klein had just given a series of lectures on "early analysis"
for which he had invited her to London, and that

she made an extraordinarily deep impression on all of us and won the highest praise both by her personality and her work. I myself have from the beginning supported her views about early analysis and although I have no direct experience of play analysis, I am inclined to account her development of it as exceedingly valuable.[Steiner 1985, p. 30]

Freud replied noncommittally that "Melanie Klein's work has aroused considerable doubt and controversy here in Vienna. I myself have no judgment on pedagogic matters" (Steiner 1985, p. 30)

Jones's next letter was an attempt to win Freud over to his enthusiastic view of Klein's work. It received this more distinctly negative reply:

To come to your remarks on child analysis. I am very glad that it has done your two little ones so much good . . . [but] I consider it unnecessary to attach too much importance to the differences between Frau Klein and Anna over technique and theory. . . .

I myself naturally endeavor to take up an attitude as far as possible impartial, because Anna is on the one hand my daughter and on the other she has written her work completely independently of me, basing it exclusively on her own experience. [Steiner 1985, p. 31]

However, he added that "the opinions of Frau Klein about the behavior of the ego ideal with children seem absolutely impossible to me and are in complete contradiction to all my basic assumptions" (p. 31). "Behavior of the ego ideal" referred to Klein's theory (the details of which are examined in Chapters 13 and 15) that the superego begins to form at a much earlier point in development than Freud's own theory indicated.

Jones protested to Freud that

As one of your chief discoveries has been the fact that young children are much more mature than had been generally supposed, both sexually and morally, I had regarded the conclusions reached from Frau Klein's experience as being

simply a direct continuation of your own tendencies. [Steiner
1985, p. 31]

Freud replied with not uncharacteristic sarcasm that "I agree with
Melanie Klein that children are much more mature than we
previously thought. But this theory has its limits and is in itself no
proof. Otherwise I would have to agree from the outset to the
assertion that children speculate on the theory of cognition" (p. 31).

Whatever Freud's estimate of Klein's work may have been, her
explorations of the unconscious minds of children eventually enabled her to devise a coherent theory of emotional and intellectual
development resting entirely on psychoanalytic methods and findings. Because she was free of the need for quasiphysical speculation
that confounded Freud's work, she was able to map the territory he
had opened without suffering qualms about the "scientific" status of
her work. She penetrated with great sensitivity and accuracy to the
"heart of the child," as Jones put it, and her discoveries there not
only confirmed Freud's basic assumptions, but showed how they
were themselves consequences of even earlier psychological processes. The result of this was a profound clarification of both the
underpinnings of psychological health, and of the nature of the most
profound psychological disturbances. Following her work, psychoanalysts for the first time were able to understand certain aspects of
psychosis, and to treat them as Freud had treated neurosis, by
attacking their roots instead of suppressing their symptoms with
drugs or suggestion (Bion 1954, 1956, 1957, 1959; Rosenfeld 1947,
1950, 1952a, 1952b, 1954, 1963; Segal 1950, 1956).

Opposition and Acceptance

Although these advances have been found extremely useful, even
indispensable, by a great many analysts, Klein's work has encountered strong opposition from many others. The latter feel that she
(and Freud) overestimated the importance of psychic reality in the
workings of the mind. This position is difficult to understand in view
of the practical therapeutic results produced by Freud's and Klein's
emphasis on the role of psychic reality in mental life, and of the

theoretical elegance and simplicity of the psychoanalytic theories that have arisen from it. The situation is made even more complex by the fact that historically much of the opposition to Klein's ideas has been opposition to distorted versions of them. The persistence of such distortions among sophisticated analysts despite her attempts to correct them is an unresolved puzzle, but its resemblance to the distortions prevalent among sophisticated Viennese physicians who were disturbed by the "many new things" that Freud found in his work with Dora is more than a little striking.

I have selected Melanie Klein's work to illustrate the development of psychoanalytic thought not because I believe that it encompasses all that has been done in psychoanalysis since Freud's death in 1939, and certainly not because it is universally accepted, but because it embodies in a crystalline way the perspective that made Freud's work into psychoanalysis. If the two of them were unscientific, as many still regard them to be, they were so in the same way; and if they were geniuses, they were geniuses at the same thing.

Despite their opposition to Klein's ideas when presented in direct or undiluted form, many American psychoanalysts have recognized that, in a practical sense, an adequate understanding of their day-to-day clinical experience with patients requires them to employ something like her discoveries. As a consequence, while her ideas as a whole have encountered strong *official* opposition from most American psychoanalysts, many of her fundamental theses are accepted under an alias, so to speak, by those who claim to oppose them.

Perhaps the most striking recent example of this appeared somewhat comically in a paper in which two prominent American psychoanalysts[1] give a number of lucid, textbook-perfect clinical examples of a type of identification first discovered and analyzed by Melanie Klein 35 years earlier. They register their disagreement with her analysis of it solely on the ground that they do not find her work "congenial." They then offer their own formulation of this "new" process, which turns out to be an unwitting paraphrase of

---

[1]Calef, V., and Weinshel, E. M. (1981). Some clinical consequences of introjection: gaslighting. *Psychoanalytic Quarterly* 50: 44–66.

Klein's. Perhaps it is best merely to take this juxtaposition of above-board opposition to her ideas and underground acceptance of them as sign of tacit, but anguished, regard.

Freud recognized the importance of psychic reality and conducted the initial scientific exploration of it. Klein in turn adapted the psychoanalytic method directly to the mind and needs of the child. Common to their work is the recognition that certain kinds of experience cannot be understood without reference to an inner world, and the conviction that the workings of psychic reality make sense and can be approached and studied in a scientific manner.

12

The Method of Child Psychoanalysis

F or more than a decade following its publication in 1909, Freud's analysis of Hans was unique. No one seriously attempted to duplicate his feat of psychoanalyzing a child, perhaps because Freud himself had warned that only in the very unusual circumstance of the child's father conducting the actual analysis, as was the case with Hans, could one hope for success. Only a father, he thought, could elicit the trust necessary for the child to divulge his wishes, dreams, and fantasies. This placed a formidable obstacle in the path of the development of child psychoanalysis as a practical procedure.

Added to this was a second objection, based on the fear that interpreting a child's unconscious wishes would unleash them in an uncontrollable form. The unquestioning acceptance of these two contradictory objections — that a child's unconscious would ordinarily be inaccessible to the analyst, and that it would be all too accessible — thoroughly chilled the development of child psychoanalysis for many years, despite the fact that in all that time no one advanced any positive evidence in support of either objection. One may nonetheless see their mark, for example, in the work of Hug-Hellmuth, who began in 1917 to explore in detail the ways in which children's spontaneous play could be used to supplement their verbal communications as means of gaining insight into their unconscious. Although she succeeded in laying some of the technical groundwork for the psychoanalysis of children, and felt that in principle psychoanalysis could offer a great deal of help to a neurotic child, she demurred from undertaking an unfettered analysis of a child for fear of stirring up repressed impulses and tendencies that the child would be unable to contain (Klein 1927a).

Klein adopted Hug-Hellmuth's technical advances in the use of play as a means of establishing contact with children, but took a position quite different from hers about the feasibility and wisdom of actually psychoanalyzing them. In 1919, she undertook her first analysis of a child, a boy of 5, and

> found (as all my later analyses confirmed) that it was perfectly possible and salutary to probe the . . . depths, and by doing so one could obtain results at least equal to those of adult analyses. But, side by side with this, I found that in an analysis so conducted not only was it unnecessary for the analyst to exert any educative influence,[1] but that the two things were incompatible. I took these discoveries as the guiding principle in my work and have advocated them in all my writings, and this is how I have come to attempt the analysis of quite little children, that is, from three to six years old, and to find it successful and full of promise. [1927a, p. 140]

In 1927, the British Psycho-Analytical Society held a symposium of child analysis intended to air these questions, to which a number of analysts, including Melanie Klein, were invited to present their views. That same year, Anna Freud, who accepted her father's admonition about the obstacle facing the psychoanalysis of children, and whose position on child psychoanalysis was generally similar to Hug-Hellmuth's, had published her book, *The Psycho-*

---

[1] By this she meant the kind of suggestion and guidance Hug-Hellmuth had advocated to mitigate the effects of analysis.

Analytical Treatment of Children. Klein presented her views at the symposium (1927a) by contrasting them with the then better-known ones of Anna Freud. She begins with an overview of the stunted state of child psychoanalysis:

> It is remarkable and should give food for thought that, though child-analysis was first attempted some eighteen years ago and has been practiced ever since, we have to face the fact that its most fundamental principles have not yet been clearly enunciated. If we compare with this fact the development of adult psychoanalysis, we shall find that, within a similar period of time, all the basic principles for the latter work were not only laid down but were empirically tested and proved beyond refutation, and that a technique was evolved the details of which had certainly to be perfected but whose fundamental principles have remained unshaken.
>
> What is the explanation that just the analysis of children should have been so much less fortunate in its development? The arguments often heard in analytical circles that children are not suitable objects for analysis does not seem to be valid . . . I think that child-analysis, as compared with that of adults, has developed so much less favorably in the past because it was not approached in a spirit of free and unprejudiced inquiry, as adult analysis was, but was hampered and burdened from the outset by certain preconceptions. [1927a, p. 141]

She lists among these preconceptions the second objection, which had been accepted without evidence by Hug-Hellmuth, Anna Freud, and many others, that a child's ego would disintegrate under the impact of a full analysis. She attempts to refute this by pointing out that it did not impede Freud at the time of his analysis of Hans:

> If we look back at that first child-analysis, the foundation of all others (that of Little Hans), we discover that it did not suffer from this limitation. Certainly there was as yet no special technique: the child's father, who carried out this partial analysis under Freud's directions, was quite unversed in the practice of analysis. In spite of this he had the courage to go quite a long way in the analysis and his results were good. . . . Freud said

that he himself would have liked to have gone further. . . .
[1927a, pp. 141–142]

Nonetheless,

> Hug-Hellmuth, who for so many years was almost alone and
> certainly pre-eminent in this field of work, [approached the
> analysis of children] from the outset with principles which were
> bound to limit it and therefore make it less fruitful, not only in
> respect of its practical results, the number of cases in which
> analysis was to be used, etc., but also in respect of theoretical
> findings. [p. 142]

As a result,

> child-analysis, which might reasonably have been expected to
> contribute directly to the development of psychoanalytical the-
> ory, has done nothing in this direction worth speaking of. Anna
> Freud, as well as Hug-Hellmuth, has the idea that in analyzing
> children we can discover not only no more, but actually *less*
> about the early period of life than when we analyze adults. . . .
> [p. 142]

She points out that if one assumes at the outset, as Anna Freud and
Hug-Hellmuth have done, that an unrestricted analysis is dangerous
for a child, and therefore refrains from attempting one, then the
testing of the question at issue—namely whether children may be
analyzed—is rendered impossible. If, on the other hand,

> one approaches child-analysis with an open mind one will
> discover ways and means of probing to the deepest depths. And
> then, from the results of the procedure one will realize what is
> the child's *true nature* and will perceive that there is no need to
> impose any restriction on the analysis, either as to the depth to
> which it may penetrate or the method by which it may work.
> [p. 142]

Klein found that, far from overwhelming a child's ego, interpretation of its unconscious impulses and fantasies strengthened it by
allowing it to know more about what it had been struggling to come
to terms with in itself even without the analysis.

Klein's Approach to the Psychoanalysis of Children

A third obstacle in the path of the analysis of children was the objection that they lacked sufficient motivation to cooperate in an analysis. This meant that since they do not as a rule feel "ill," they will not make the effort needed to follow the "fundamental rule" of free association. According to this line of reasoning, children would need a nonanalytic inducement to "divulge their secrets" to the analyst.

Klein realized that this objection rested on two misconceptions. The first is about the nature of free association. It does not consist of divulging secrets — that is, communicating what one has consciously withheld. It consists of reporting spontaneously what appears in one's mind. The second misconception is about the degree of conscious cooperation required from a child for analysis to proceed. Although adults may need to make an effort to free-associate, so to speak, children seem to do so naturally. Their conscious willingness is therefore not required. In Klein's first published paper (1921), she observes that children *spontaneously* elaborate verbal fantasies that sound like the dreams of adults, and that they seem to regard playing and telling of fantasies as equivalent, interchangeable activities. Further experience with children confirmed the impression that play, verbal fantasies, and dreams all had equivalent psychological significance for children. This meant that play and verbal fantasies could be used in their analyses in precisely the way that Freud had used Dora's dreams and free associations in her analysis.

Communication about their unconscious through play was an activity for which children, who make much less of a distinction between their conscious and unconscious minds than do adults, need no special motivation. Their natural capacity for play and the spontaneous expression of fantasy renders possible the kind of contact with the unconscious that an adult can achieve only by the effort of free association. Once this is seen, the third objection melts away.

Within a few years, Klein developed an approach to the psychoanalysis of children that was remarkably similar to that which Freud had developed for adults. She interpreted all the various manifestations of resistance (which, it will be recalled, Freud had identified as the hallmark of the analysis having come near a repressed idea), and she also freely interpreted the transference (which Freud had regarded as the most effective way of bringing to consciousness repressed ideas and emotions). Moreover, she gauged the accuracy of her interpretations not merely by the child's assent or disagreement, but by the interpretation's effectiveness in diminishing anxiety, in enabling the child to play and communicate more freely, in deepening the child's relationship in the transference to the analysis, and in aiding the child to establish a deeper and more realistic relationship with the people in his or her life. These are precisely the criteria used by Freud (and still used today) for assessing the accuracy of interpretations in the analysis of adults. Klein's establishing analytic contact with children in a manner identical in form, if not in details, to that used by Freud with adults, provides striking evidence that analysis is literally and not just metaphorically a way of making contact with the child inside an adult.

In a paper called "The Psychological Principles of Early Analysis" (1926), Klein emphasized these similarities between her approach and that already established with adults:

> It is a question only of a difference of *technique*, not of the *principles* of treatment. The criteria of the psychoanalytic method proposed by Freud, namely, that we should use as our starting point the facts of transference and resistance, [and] that we should take into account infantile impulses, repression and its effects, amnesia and the compulsion to repetition . . . all these criteria are maintained in their entirety in the play technique. The method of play preserved all the principles of psychoanalysis and leads to the same results as the classic technique. Only it is adapted to the minds of children in the technical means employed. [p. 138]

On one side of this debate over the feasibility of psychoanalyzing children is Klein, explaining what she has done and how she did it, and on the other is Anna Freud, saying it can't be done. Charcot would have enjoyed this clash between theoretical prediction and factual evidence. By daring to put the possibility of an unfettered analysis of a child to the test, Klein acted in accordance with the determination Freud expressed in his discussion of Hans, not to be "bound by the prejudices of our ignorance."

Eventually, as Anna Freud gathered more experience in the psychoanalysis of children (as distinct from the combination of analysis and suggestion that she had started out using), and as her practice became more solidly based on analytic principles, her conclusions about its feasibility and suitability came more into line with Klein's.

Klein's Technique of Child Analysis

The technical procedure that Klein developed for the psychoanalysis of children followed from her conviction that, since the object of psychoanalysis is to form a link with the patient's unconscious, and since the unconscious of children and of adults do not differ in essence, children may and should be psychoanalyzed according to the same principles that govern the analyses of adults. She equipped a room with a low table on which were placed a number of small and simple toys:

> . . . little wooden men and women, usually in two sizes, cars, wheelbarrows, swings, aeroplanes, animals, trees, bricks, houses, fences, paper, scissors, a knife, pencils, chalks or paints, glue, balls and marbles, plasticine and string. The room itself had a washable floor, running water, a few chairs, a little sofa, some cushions and a chest of drawers. [It was] essential to have *small* toys because their number and variety enable the child to express a wide range of phantasies and experiences . . . Their very simplicity enables the child to use them in many different situations, according to the material coming up in his play. . . . The play-room . . . does not contain anything except what is needed for psychoanalysis. [1955, p. 126]

The small and nonsuggestive toys lend themselves readily to adoption by a variety of fantasies and wishes. The play, like free association, is intended above all to be free of any influence or suggestion by the analyst, and the entire setting, from the structure of the room to the details of the toys, is designed to facilitate the child's equivalent of free association: free play, limited only by realistic considerations of safety.

Of greater importance than the physical setting, however, was the psychological setting created by the analyst.

> The games I have described, through which the child [communicates] . . . differ greatly from the games which children are usually observed to play. This is to be explained as follows: The analyst gets his material in a very specific way. The attitude he shows to the child's associations and games is entirely free from ethical and moral criticism. This is indeed one of the ways in which a transference can be established and analysis set going. Thus the child will show to the analyst what it never would reveal to its mother or nurse. For good reasons: as they would be very much shocked to notice aggression and unsocial tendencies against which [their efforts are] mostly directed. Moreover, it is just the analytical work which resolves repressions and in this way brings about the manifestations of the unconscious [the prevalence of which is precisely what makes the play seen in analysis differ from that observed in other settings]. [1927b, p. 175]

Transference in Children

The fourth and final objection against the psychoanalysis of children that Klein had to answer was the idea that, since they are still strongly tied to their parents, children are unable to form a transference to the analyst. This objection, too, was based on a misunderstanding, in this case one about the nature of transference.

Klein realized this shortly after beginning her work with children in the psychoanalytic setting, when she found that they would often assign her a role to play in their games, and that the role varied according to the child's mood and general frame of mind. By comparing these roles and the child's state of mind at the time, she concluded that they were representations of parts of the child's inner world, and in particular of the child's superego. For a child, play was a way of putting a certain aspect of the mind into the external world. The technical term for this is *projection*.

She saw that the purpose of these projections was to relieve the pressure of a conflict in the child's internal world. By means of projection, an intrapsychic conflict is spread into the external world, and thereby becomes less intense, violent, and painful. The child obtains some relief from conflicts, and the analysis also benefits: By experiencing the roles he is given to play, the analyst gains first-hand experience of what the child's inner world is like. The resemblance between this recruitment of the analyst into the child's games and fantasies, and the involvement of the analyst in the adult patient's unconscious fantasies in the transference, is no coincidence. The projection of a part of the patient's mind into the analyst that Klein observed in children is the unconscious basis of transference itself. The existence of transference in children was one of the first discoveries of child analysis.

These "personifications in play," as she called them — the child's version of transference — follow the same rules that transferences do in the unconscious of adults. Her identification of transference in children, the fulcrum on which analysis rests, put their analyses on a footing identical to that of adults and removed the objection that children cannot be analyzed because they cannot form a transference. The misunderstanding on which this objection was based was the idea that transference is a "revival" of a strictly historical relationship, somehow experienced as a current reality, and that children — still being involved in the primary relationship with their parents — have no past relationships to revive.

Klein saw that transference was not the resurrection of a superseded relationship, but a projection of a part of the child's *current* unconscious inner world; not a dead relationship with one's parents artificially revived in analysis, but an externalization (via projection) of a live, unconscious one. Insofar as the patient's transference relationship to the analyst is a present-day version of an earlier relationship with the parents, it is because the forces that constituted the patient's contribution to the early relationship are still active in the patient's unconscious. There, they continue to mold all his current relationships, of which transference is only one

example, although an especially well-studied one. The analysis gives
these forces a stage on which they may play, and their impact on the
analytic situation is what gives the transference relationship the
character of a unique psychological fingerprint.

The patient's past relationship to parents and current transference relationship to the analyst are not cause and effect, then, but
samples of the same thing occurring at two different times. What is
constant over time are the patient's unconscious ways of relating to
objects that originated in the past and persist into the present. This
is also true of children, whose transference is a continuation of their
modes of relating to their parents in infancy.

Children are not only able to form a transference with the
analyst, but, thanks to their proficiency at projecting parts of their
inner world into the outside world (a process that forms an
important basis of meaningful play), they are extremely adept at
doing so. The evolution of the transference is a living biopsy of how
children formed their relationship to their parents. By observing it
in adults or children, the analyst is freed from having to rely
exclusively on reports of the patient's history; he can see history
repeating itself with his own eyes.

Klein also noted that a child would assign a role openly in play
to the analyst only if it was a positive one — that is, if the transference
was positive. But if the role — the predominant transference — was a
hostile or negative one, the child was much more reluctant to assign
it openly — to acknowledge it. This place a much greater demand on
the analyst's intuition and emotional resources if he is to identify the
transference. But for the analysis to be complete, both the positive
and the negative transferences must be brought to light. Her
recommendation for the management of transference in children is
therefore a repetition of the even-handed one Freud made for adults
at the time of "Dora":

> What is true of personification in its open form I have also found
> to be indispensable for the more disguised and obscure [nega-
> tive] forms of the personifications underlying transference. The
> analyst who wishes . . . to strike at the roots of the super-ego's
> severity, must have no preference for any particular role; he
> must accept that which comes to him from the analytic situation.
> [1929, p. 209]

The link uniting her approach to the child's unconscious with Freud's approach to the adult's is a common attitude toward the patient's mind. Klein concluded her contribution to the 1927 symposium by stressing the analytic attitude that underlies this unity:

> What we have to do with children as well as with adults is not simply to establish and maintain the analytic situation by every analytic means and refrain from all *direct* educative[2] influence, but, more than that, a children's analyst must have the same unconscious attitude as we require in the analyst of adults, if he is to be successful. It must enable him to be really willing *only to analyze* and not to wish to mold and direct the minds of his patients. If anxiety does not prevent him, he will be able calmly to wait for the development of the correct issue, and in this way that issue will be achieved. [1927a, p. 167]

---

[2] By "educative" Klein meant not what present-day Americans mean by the word, but rather something that would correspond to our idea of behavior modification: the shaping of the child's emotional states by means of punishment and reward.

13

The Child's Construction of Experience

Melanie Klein's earliest psychological interests centered on the question of children's intellectual development — how they come to think for themselves, develop critical judgment, and learn from their own experiences. This led her to the problem of what inhibited such development. Like Freud in his first efforts to solve the problem of neurosis, Klein believed that the source of the problem must be environmental, and that if children could be given an environment in which their curiosity was encouraged in all possible ways, their intellectual potential would be fully realized. Accordingly, her first therapeutic contact with a child was an experiment directed at making the child's environment more conducive to emotional and intellectual development by eliminating all influences that might repress healthy curiosity.

External Repression

She reported the results of her experiment in a paper, "The Development of a Child" (Klein 1921), which she read before the Hungarian Psychoanalytical Society in 1919, in which she emphasized the devastating effects of a repressive environment on a child's development:

> We are apt to lay stress on the "courage" of the thinker who, in opposition to usage and authority, succeeds in carrying out entirely original researches. It would not require so much "courage" if it were not that [as children the researchers needed] a quite peculiar spirit to think out for themselves, in opposition to the highest authorities, the ticklish subjects which are in part denied, in part forbidden. . . . How much of an individual's intellectual equipment is only apparently his own, how much is dogmatic, theoretic and due to authority, not achieved for himself by his own free, unhampered thought! [1921, p. 22]

This early awareness of the toll exacted on children by external repression never flagged throughout her long career. But further experience showed that even when external obstacles were removed as far as possible, the child's intellectual development might still remain quite inhibited in certain areas. She also saw that while one child may be hampered greatly by a certain kind of external repression, another might be affected relatively little. She drew from these observations the conviction that there must be some additional factor that needed to be taken into account, an *internal* one, working either on its own or in conjunction with external events, to repress the child's curiosity. The title of her second paper, written two years after the first, was "The Child's Resistance to Enlightenment."[1]

In this paper, she described in detailed, naturalistic terms her observations of the child's words and behavior, from which she surmised that certain children with inhibited development had somehow unconsciously equated learning with sexual or aggressive activities. When the impulses associated with the latter are re-

---

[1]The two were published together in 1921 under the title of the first.

pressed, for example as a result of oedipal conflicts, the learning that is connected to them in the child's mind is also repressed. This meant that even the most enlightened upbringing was not enough to ensure that the child's full developmental potential would be realized in all cases, since oedipal conflicts arise even in the most enlightened environments. Children who were unable to work them through suffered internal inhibitions of their development, and would therefore benefit only by an approach directed internally. Psychoanalysis offered such an approach, and Klein's development of a practical technique for psychoanalyzing children was motivated in part by her desire to find a way of removing these internal inhibitions.

She recounts her first attempt to do so in these somewhat harrowing terms:

My first patient was a five-year-old boy. . . . To begin with I thought it would be sufficient to influence the mother's attitude. I suggested that she should encourage the child to discuss freely with her the many unspoken questions which were obviously at the back of his mind and were impeding his intellectual development. This had a good effect, but his neurotic difficulties were not sufficiently alleviated and it was soon decided I should psychoanalyze him. In doing so . . . I interpreted what I thought to be most urgent in the material the child presented to me and found my interest focussing on his anxieties and the defenses against them. This new approach soon confronted me with serious problems. The anxieties I encountered when analyzing this first case were very acute, and although I was strengthened in the belief that I was working on the right lines by observing the alleviation again and again produced by my interpretations, I was at times perturbed by the intensity of the fresh anxieties that were being brought into the open. On one such occasion I sought advice from Dr. Karl Abraham. He replied that since my interpretations up to then had produced relief and the analysis was obviously progressing, he saw no grounds for changing the method of approach. I felt encouraged by his support and, as it happened, in the next few days the child's anxiety, which had come to a head, greatly diminished, leading to further improvement. The conviction gained in this analysis strongly influenced the whole course of my analytic work. [1955, pp. 122–123]

Her confidence was further reinforced by her experience with another of her early cases, a quite disturbed, very young girl of 2 years and 9 months, whom she called Rita. Rita suffered from

> night terrors and animal phobias, [and] was very ambivalent toward her mother, at the same time clinging to her to such an extent that she could hardly be left alone. She had a marked obsessional neurosis and was at times very depressed. Her play was inhibited and her inability to tolerate frustrations made her upbringing increasingly difficult. [1955, p. 124]

At first, Klein was

> very doubtful about how to tackle this case since the analysis of so young a child was an entirely new experiment. The first session seemed to confirm my misgivings. Rita, when left alone with me in her nursery, at once showed signs of what I took to be a negative transference: she was anxious and silent and very soon asked to go out into the garden. I agreed and went with her—I may add, under the watchful eyes of her mother and aunt, who took this as a sign of failure. They were very surprised to see that Rita was quite friendly towards me when we returned to the nursery some ten to fifteen minutes later. The explanation of this change was that while we were outside I had been interpreting her negative transference. . . . From a few things she said, and the fact that she was less frightened when we were out in the open, I concluded that she was particularly afraid of something I might do to her when she was alone with me in the room. I interpreted this, and, referring to her night terrors, I linked her suspicion of me as a hostile stranger with her fear that a bad woman would attack her when she was by herself at night. When, a few minutes after this interpretation, I suggested that we should return to the nursery, she readily agreed. . . . This case strengthened my growing conviction that a precondition for the psychoanalysis of a child is to understand and interpret the phantasies, feelings, anxieties and experiences expressed in play, or, if play activities are inhibited, the causes of inhibition. [1955, p. 124]

Although the interpretation of a child's unconscious anxieties provided genuine relief, Klein's child patients tended to respond to it by producing new anxieties and fantasies, some of them quite alarming. She wondered if these new anxieties had been caused by her interpretations, but soon recognized from their content that they had existed before in a latent form, and were in fact what had underlain her patients' symptoms and inhibitions all along. Her interpretations, which were directed at anxieties relatively close to the surface, were simultaneously relieving them and (perhaps even as a *result* of relieving them) allowing deeper ones to emerge, which the child could now experience more consciously, and thereby express not as symptoms but as fantasies. Her interpretations led her "deeper and deeper into the unconscious and into the phantasy life of the child . . [and] opened up the understanding of early infantile phantasies, anxieties and defenses, which were at that time largely unexplored" (pp. 132–133).

The Child's Internal World

Klein found that in the course of their analyses children would express vivid fantasies reflecting unconscious impulses and figures as terrifying, or, alternatively, as gratifying, as any found in the unexpurgated Grimm.[2] These unconscious fantasies, of an extreme and shifting nature, corresponded to the equally extreme and rapidly shifting emotions that are part of every infant's and small child's makeup.

> The young infant, without being able to grasp it intellectually, feels every discomfort as though it were inflicted by hostile forces. If comfort is given to him soon—in particular warmth, the loving way he is held, and the gratification of being fed—this gives rise to happier emotions. Such comfort is felt to come from good forces and, I believe, makes possible the infant's first loving relationship to a person. . . . [1959, p. 248]

---

[2]This sheds some light, incidentally, on the fascination that these tales, even grisly ones, have for children. They correspond absorbingly to the content of their unconscious minds.

How do these infantile constructions of experience — events being caused by good and bad forces — arise? The first suggestion of an answer came from Klein's observations of her young patients' violent reactions to the frustrations they experienced at the hands of their parents. Among these reactions were vivid fantasies of mutilation of the parents' eyes, genitals, and insides by biting, tearing, burning, and poisoning; of having the two parents tear each other to pieces while they were in bed together; and of locking them up in a house while setting fire to it so they would "burst."

Klein herself seems to have been stunned by the extravagant violence of these reactions, and by the early age at which they seemed, in her analytic reconstructions, to have occurred:

> The idea of an infant of from six to twelve months trying to destroy its mother by every method at the disposal of its sadistic trends — with its teeth, nails and excreta and with the whole of its body, transformed in fantasy into all kinds of dangerous weapons — presents a horrifying, not to say an unbelievable picture to our minds. And it is difficult, I know from my own experience, to bring oneself to recognize that such an abhorrent idea answers to the truth. But the abundance, force and multiplicity of the cruel fantasies which accompany these cravings are displayed before our eyes in early analyses so clearly and forcibly that they leave no room for doubt. [1932, p. 130]

After the initial shock of what she had discovered in the minds of her young patients had worn off, she realized that

> we cannot apply any ethical standards to these impulses; we have to take their existence for granted, without any criticism, and help the child to deal with them; whereby we at the same time diminish his sufferings, strengthen his capacities, his mental equilibrium, and in the final result accomplish a work of notable social importance. [1927b, p. 176]

A second clue to the formation of these infantile experiences came from the small child's equally extravagant capacity for devotion:

I must say that the impression I get of the way in which even the quite small child fights his unsocial tendencies is rather touching and impressive. One moment after we have seen the most sadistic impulses, we meet with performances showing the greatest capacity for love and the wish to make all possible sacrifices to be loved. [1927b, p. 176]

Klein believed that every infant forms such a positive relationship with its mother at the earliest stage of life, and that this relationship is vital to its physical and psychological survival:

My hypothesis is that the infant has an innate unconscious awareness of the existence of the mother. We know that young animals at once turn to the mother and find their food from her. The human animal is not different in that respect, and this instinctual knowledge is the basis for the infant's primal relation to his mother. We can also observe that at an age of only a few weeks the baby already looks up to his mother's face, recognizes her footsteps, the touch of her hands, the smell and feel of her breast or of the bottle that she gives him, all of which suggests that some relation, however primitive, to the mother has been established. [1959, p. 248]

Remnants of this loving and life-sustaining relationship with the mother are present in the unconscious of every child, even those who show no overt sign 'of it, as she found in her analysis of Peter, a 12-year-old delinquent boy who appeared entirely devoid of the capacity to love (1927b). His father had died during the war, and soon after, his mother developed a fatal cancer. He was in the charge of an older sister who abused him and "forced him and his smaller brother at a very early age to sexual acts." His mother eventually died, and he was transferred to a series of foster mothers, under whose care he grew progressively worse. At this point his delinquency emerged, which consisted of "breaking open the school cupboard and a tendency to steal in general, but mostly breaking up things, and sexual attacks on little girls. He had no relationship to anyone but a destructive one; his boy friendships had mostly this purpose too. He had no special interest and even seemed indifferent to punishment and rewards" (1927b, p. 181).

Surprisingly, her attempts to form an analytic relationship with this boy were successful, a fact she accounts for by observing that

> a child does not need special motives for analysis; it is a question of technical measures to establish the transference and keep the analysis going. *I do not believe in the existence of a child in whom it is impossible to obtain this transference, in whom the capacity for love cannot be brought out.* In the case of my little criminal, he was apparently devoid of any capacity for love, but analysis proved that this was not so. He had a good transference to me, good enough to make analysis possible, although he had no motives for it, since he even did not show any special aversion to being sent to the reformatory. Moreover, the analysis showed that this dull boy had a deep and sincere love for his mother. The mother died in terrible circumstances from cancer, which in the last stage led to complete decay. The daughter did not like to go near her, and it was *he* who looked after her. As she lay dead, the family was leaving [their home]. He could not be found for some time: he had locked himself up with his dead mother in the room. [1927b, pp. 184–185]

The extreme polarity between boundless love and sadistic hatred that Klein found in the unconscious fantasies and emotional lives of her small patients, and the titanic conflict between the two in even the youngest ones, have profound implications for our understanding of how children — and in their unconscious, adults — construe their experiences. She comments that

> although psychology and pedagogy have always maintained the belief that a child is a happy being without any conflicts, and have assumed that the sufferings of adults are the results of the burdens and hardships of reality, it must be asserted that *just the opposite is true.* What we learn about the child and the adult through psychoanalysis shows that all the sufferings of later life are for the most part repetitions of these earlier ones, and that every child in the first years of life goes through an immeasurable degree of suffering. [1927b, p. 173]

Klein found from her analyses that the life of small children is literally dominated by their psychic reality: Their loving and sadistic fantasies and impulses, and derivatives of these, all form a complex inner matrix out of which the rest of their mental and emotional life evolves. The picture that children form of the external world is not exempt from this dominance by their fantasies and impulses, and it is this that explains the fantastic character of their experiences.

What had started out as an assumption that children's development or maldevelopment was environmentally determined had become an investigation whose results showed that children's early development was heavily dependent on the impact of their own fantasies and psychic reality, and that the further back one probed, the more this was so. This raised the problem of how unconscious fantasies could play such a prominent role in so early a stage of mental development. The rather informal theoretical formulation of unconscious fantasy that had sufficed for Freud was already being strained by the specific new data arising from the analyses of children. A more rigorous formulation based on this new information was now required.

14

Instinct, Fantasy, and Early Psychic Processes

Fantasy and Instinct

Freud believed that the mind's simplest, most primitive, and most direct response to an instinctual urge was an unconscious fantasy that represents the urge as magically satisfied. Such fantasies arise in infancy, and continue to be produced in the unconscious throughout life, forming, for example, the latent content of dreams. He called the processes that produce these fantasies the "primary process," a name he chose because it indicates that they are among the earliest of the mind's operations. In his view, the infant's mental life consisted almost entirely of such processes. A baby's innate, primary process response to hunger, for example, is "hallucinatory gratification"—a fantasy of fullness so forceful and vivid that it is experienced as absolutely real, like the events in a hallucination or a dream.

Although Freud had been forced by clinical experience to hold his physiologic model in abeyance when it came to adults or older children, he still applied it to the area of mental life most remote from his clincal experience, that of infancy. Accordingly, he looked at "primary processes" from a physiologic point of view. For him, they were primitive, premental, physiological mechanisms that facilitated the discharge of instinctual tensions from the nervous apparatus.

Freud never tried to locate precisely the dividing line between the neurophysiology of the young infant and the psychology of the child because it was not a pressing clinical issue for him. Concerned only with the analysis of adults, he could leave the problem of the earliest stages of mental life unresolved. He was therefore free to continue to believe in his physiology as long as he restricted himself to the *terra incognita* of infancy, much as the composers of medieval bestiaries were free to locate their fabulous beasts in remote areas of the world. But because the analysis of children touched very closely on these early stages of mental life, Klein was forced to face directly the question of the infant's actual experience. Her solution was remarkably simple. She assumed, as a working hypothesis, that the relationship Freud had established between instinctual urges and the type of unconscious fantasies associated with latent dream content in the adult applies from the very beginning of life: Instinctual urges give rise to something like emotion-laden fantasies even in young infants, who therefore have a mental life, composed largely of vivid, concrete fantasies. This state of mind would, like dreaming, be located somewhere between hallucination and contact with the external world.

Her colleague Isaacs (1952) summarized her view of the relationship between unconscious fantasy and instinct most concisely:

> Phantasy is (in the first instance) the mental corollary, the psychic representative of instinct. There is no impulse, no instinctual urge which is not experienced as unconscious phantasy. . . . [Moreover], the particular content of the urges or feelings (for example, wishes, fears, anxieties, triumphs, love or sorrow) dominating the mind at the moment [is also represented by a fantasy]. [p. 83]

In speaking of instinctual urges, one is speaking, as far as the mind is concerned, of unconscious fantasy. The same is true of emotions: What we call emotional states are at bottom unconscious fantasies.

By characterizing these states of mind as unconscious fantasies, Klein meant there was an unbroken continuum between even the most primitive of them, on one hand, and what we recognize as elaborate and sophisticated conscious fantasy on the other. Describing these very early fantasies and mental states is quite difficult, however, as Klein recognized:

> When these pre-verbal emotions and phantasies are revived in the transference situation, they appear as "memories in feelings," as I would call them, and are reconstructed and put into words with the help of the analyst. In the same way, words have to be used when we are reconstructing and describing other phenomena belonging to the early stages of development. In fact we cannot translate the language of the unconscious into consciousness without lending it words from our conscious realm . . . All this is felt by the infant in much more primitive ways than language can express. [1957, p. 180n]

This point has been subject to confusion. Some have mistaken her to mean that infants are capable of the complex and sophisticated fantasies found in adults. In fact, she knew that the latter are the product of a long process of development that originates in the primitive fantasies she is trying to describe. Primitive fantasies are experienced in concrete terms, more as somatic sensations than as abstract images. The more primitive the fantasy, the more it is experienced as a somatic sensation. The feelings contained in a young infant's impulses and emotions are hardly distinguishable from bodily feelings. Our use of the same English term to describe both types of experience reflects their original indistinguishability.

Unconscious Fantasy and External Reality

Fantasies feed into the infant's perceptions and sensations, thereby endowing even the most elementary of them with psychological significance. Klein felt it would be a mistake to

assume that the breast is to [the infant] merely a physical object.
The whole of his instinctual desires and his unconscious phantasies imbue the breast with qualities going far beyond the actual
nourishment it affords.

   We find in our analyses of our patients that the breast in its
[gratifying] aspect is the prototype of maternal goodness, inexhaustible patience and generosity, as well as of creativeness. It is
these phantasies and instinctual needs that so enrich the primal
object [i.e., the breast] that it remains the foundation for hope,
trust and belief in goodness. [1957, p. 180]

Infants animate their gratifying experience with the breast by
imbuing it with their own vital impulses, in the form of unconscious
fantasies that make physical satisfaction psychologically meaningful
by meeting it halfway. This process converts physical gratification
from a raw (inanimate) sensation into a rudimentary experience of
a generous, loving (and animate) mother. Klein filled out Freud's
theory of the life instinct by suggesting that it expresses itself in the
form of unconscious loving fantasies that animate experiences of
satisfaction, making them psychologically meaningful.

   Just as the infant brings positive experiences to psychological
life by endowing them with certain unconscious fantasies, the same
occurs with painful sensations:

   The child's earliest experiences of painful external and internal
   stimuli provide a basis for phantasies about hostile external and
   internal objects, and they contribute largely to the building up of
   such phantasies. In the earliest stages of mental development
   every unpleasant stimulus is apparently related in the baby's
   phantasy to the "hostile" or denying breasts. . . . [1936, p. 292]

As the mother who gratifies the infant becomes the object of the
infant's primitive loving feelings and fantasies, and thereby becomes
not just gratifying but loving and "good," the frustrating, "hostile"
mother incurs the infant's hatred and becomes the target of vivid
destructive fantasies, which makes her not just frustrating but
malevolent and "bad."

   Even in the first months of life, the infant's mind is dominated by profound impulses of love and hatred (whose discovery in young children was described in Chapter 13) and their corollary fantasies, experienced in the most vivid way, all fluctuating in accordance with the infant's momentary states of security or insecurity, need or gratification. Klein wrote that she

> recognized, in watching the constant struggle in the young infant's mental processes between an irrepressible urge to destroy as well as to save himself, to attack his objects and to preserve them, that primordial forces struggling with each other were at work. This gave me a deeper insight into the vital *clinical* importance of Freud's concept of life and death instincts. [1958, p. 236]

Fantasy and Psychological Structure

Unconscious fantasies are also responsible in part for building up the structure of the mind itself. In "Mourning and Melancholia," Freud described how a lost object is installed in the ego as the result of an "oral impulse," a process he called incorporation. Klein assumed that this impulse must have a fantasy representative, in however rudimentary a form, from the beginning of life. Children represent these fantasies and their psychological consequences in their play, as in the case of the 4-year-old boy making paper snowflakes and pretending to eat them, who suddenly stopped and asked, with a worried look, whether people who swallowed snowflakes would melt. Once ingested in fantasy, the object is felt to reside inside one as an "internal object," being affected by one, and affecting one in return, in the ways suggested by the boy's question. The many repetitions and permutations of these experiences contribute to a building-up of a world of concretely experienced internal objects. Klein called this unconscious fantasy "introjection."

Complementing introjection is projection, its reverse, which is based on an unconscious fantasy of excretion. As introjection, through fantasies of ingestion, leads us to experience ourselves as having taken an external object inside ourselves, so projection, acting through fantasies of physical excretion, makes us experience some quality of ourselves as residing outside in an external object.

In line with Freud's view about the role of identification in the establishment of the superego and the growth of the ego (Chapter 8), Klein believed that the inner world (which is what the technical terms *ego* and *superego* refer to) is a collection of identifications based on introjection. But as Freud saw in "Mourning and Melancholia," the building up of the inner world depends not just on taking in the outer one, but also on the alteration to which the outer one is first subjected by projection. Projection acts to color the outer world and thus influences the infant's experience of what may be taken in by introjection. Loving impulses tend to produce an experience of a "good" object and hating impulses of a "bad" one.

The endowment of an infant's perceptions of the external world with the infant's own loving and hating impulses occurs by means of projection, the capacity for which is innate. To put it in terms of Bion's patient, discussed in Chapter 1, projection enables us to experience in the outer world such psychological qualities as the "love, solace and understanding" that, in addition to physical gratification, are necessary for mental survival.

Introjection in turn fosters the gradual development of a concretely experienced inner world, consisting of the aspects of the outer world that have been "swallowed" and are therefore felt to exist within one. The inner world is formed in the image of the outer one, albeit an image that has been altered in important ways by the process of projection:

> The baby, having incorporated his parents, feels them to be live people inside his body in the concrete way in which deep unconscious fantasies are experienced—they are, in his mind, "internal" or "inner" objects, as I have termed them. Thus an inner world is being built up in the child's unconscious mind, corresponding to his actual experiences and the impression he gains from people and the external world, and yet altered by his own phantasies and impulses. . . . In the baby's mind, the "internal" mother is bound up with the "external" one, of whom she is a "double," though one which at once undergoes alterations in his mind through the very process of internalization; that is to say, his image is influenced by his phantasies, and by

internal stimuli and internal experiences of all kinds. When external situations which he lives through become internalized — and I hold that they do, from the earliest days onwards — they follow the same pattern: they also become "doubles" of real situations, and are again altered for the same reasons. [1940, pp. 345-346]

The consequences of the interplay between projection and introjection are manifested in what we call our states of mind:

The specific system of phantasies centering on the internal world is of supreme importance for the development of the ego. The internalized objects are felt by the young infant to have a life of their own, harmonizing or conflicting with each other and with the ego, according to the infant's emotions and experiences. When the infant feels he contains good objects, he experiences trust, confidence and security. When he feels he contains bad objects, he experiences persecution and suspicion. [1952, pp. 58-59]

This is worth pausing for a moment to consider. It means that what we refer to as a feeling or mood of trust, confidence, and security, for example, are simply vivid unconscious fantasies of containing a sturdy, good object living inside us. This applies equally to the mind of the infant, the unconscious of Bion's patient, and that of any other adult.

Introjection and projection are themselves fantasy representatives of oral and anal instinctual impulses that operate from the beginning of life. They are therefore among the earliest psychic processes. One might say that on its most primitive level, the mind acts like an alimentary tract, ingesting and excreting various objects as though they were psychic substances. Klein believed that it is the balanced interplay of projection and introjection that produces, from the beginning of life, the dreamlike melding of internal and external reality that Freud discovered over and over to be the modus operandi of the unconscious. She could now also add that the same process is responsible for animating experience and making it psychologically meaningful.

Because the internal world also originates partly from the

child's perception of the external one, the nature of the child's external world plays an important role in shaping the internal one.

> The object-world of the child in the first two to three months of its life could be described as consisting of hostile and persecuting, or else of gratifying parts and portions of the real world. Before long the child perceives more and more of the whole person of the mother, and this more realistic perception extends to the whole world beyond the mother. The fact that a good relation to its mother and to the external world helps the baby to overcome its early paranoid anxieties throws a new light on the importance of its earliest experiences. From its inception analysis has always laid stress on the importance of the child's early experiences, but it seems to me that only since we know more about the nature and contents of its early anxieties, and the continuous interplay between its actual experiences and its phantasy-life, can we fully understand *why* the external factor is so important. [1935, p. 285]

The child's outer world is a factor in psychological development precisely to the extent that it contributes to the ultimate structure of the inner world. This contribution is, however, mitigated by the fantasy-coloring injected into actual experiences by the infant. We recognize this when we speak of each individual's unique response to experience. It is the interplay between fantasy and external experiences (via the operation of introjection and projection) that leads to the gradual alteration and building up of the inner world, in a manner unique to each person, and that constitutes an individual's psychological and emotional development.

15

Projective Identification and the Formation of the Inner World

The Formation of the Superego

After completing his painful reappraisal of neurotic anxiety and neurotic symptom formation in *Inhibitions, Symptoms and Anxiety,* Freud concluded that neurotic symptoms were a defense against neurotic anxiety, and that neurotic anxiety was in turn produced by threats against the patient emanating from his superego. This turned the problem of neurosis on its head. It was not that repression produced anxiety by damming up libido. It was that anxiety produced repression. Neurosis was the product of a hostile superego, and psychoanalysts now had to seek out what made the superego so threatening. To do so, they needed to study its development, and this now became the focal point of research into neurosis.

Based on the data he obtained from his analyses of adults, Freud's reconstruction of the psychological events of childhood indicated that the superego first arose as a consequence of the resolution of the Oedipus complex at age 4 or 5. He was, of course, aware of certain clinical facts that did not fit in well with this model; for example, the destructiveness and cruelty of the superego found in the type of patient most resistant to his attempts at analysis, the "moral masochist," marked it as having formed sometime before the Oedipus complex, in the anal period of 1 to 2 years of age. But such a phenomenon appeared to be present only in rare or extreme cases whose existence needn't call into question the theory that the superego formed at the resolution of the Oedipus complex. This still appeared to be an adequate description for the vast majority of adult cases.

The theory that the superego originated at age 4 or 5 remained a cornerstone of Freud's model of personality structure, until Klein's direct psychoanalytic studies of children showed that a superego was regularly to be found in children well before the age of 4 or 5. For example, Klein's patient Rita, whom we encountered in Chapter 13,

> used to play the role of a severe and punishing mother who treated her child (represented by the doll and myself) very cruelly. Furthermore, her ambivalence toward her mother, her extreme need to be punished, her feelings of guilt and her night terrors led me to recognize that in this child aged two years and nine months—and quite clearly going back to a much earlier age—a harsh and relentless super-ego operated. I found this discovery confirmed in the analyses of other young children and came to the conclusion that the super-ego arises at a much earlier stage than Freud assumed. In other words, it became clear to me that the super-ego, as conceived by him, is the end product of a development which extends over years. [1955, p. 133]

Klein concluded that

> there could be no doubt that a super-ego had been in full operation for some time in my small patients of between two and three-quarters and four years of age, whereas according to the accepted view the super-ego would not begin to be activated until the Oedipus complex had died down—i.e. until about the

fifth year of life. Furthermore, my data showed that the super-ego was immeasurably harsher and more cruel than that of the older child or adult, and that it literally crushed down the feeble ego of the small child. [1933, p. 248]

Everyday observation confirms these analytic findings: Children of age 2 or 3 display a fierce morality in their play with dolls, pets, or each other that suggests a superego of great severity.

The discovery that the superego not only existed as a powerful intrapsychic agency prior to the resolution of the Oedipus complex shattered Freud's Oedipal theory of the origin of the superego. In doing so, it raised a pressing question: If the superego was already in force long before the Oedipus complex which was supposed to have been its source, how did it arise? A second question also arose from Klein's clinical findings about the early superego: Why was it so harsh? Since the problem of neurosis now seemed more and more to collapse into that of the harshness of the superego, questions about the origins and character of the superego had great clinical and theoretical importance. Since the harsh superego seemed, at least in some cases, to be a creature of early childhood, research into the origins of neurosis now shifted to the study of that period.

It was apparent from the first that there was a major difference between the superego that existed in early childhood and the later one Freud had detected at the resolution of the Oedipus complex. In its later form, the superego makes itself known by producing guilt, while the early superego produced not guilt but terror and extreme anxiety. In this respect, the superego of a normal adult resembled the later one, while the neurotic's superego resembled the early one of the infant.

Klein pointed out that the early superego's character — so monstrous, destructive, and cruel — made it unlikely that it could be based entirely on the infant's experience of actual parental behavior. This offered support for her hypothesis that unconscious fantasies, expressing both loving and hating impulses, enter into the infant's experience of the parents and alter it in profound ways. The superegos of infants, she concluded, should be regarded as an amalgam of experience and instinct-laden unconscious fantasy.

This amounts to no more than saying that the relationship

between the superego and the infant's external parents was the same that Freud had discovered in 1897 between his hysterical patients' unconscious "memory" of seduction and the external events of their childhoods. In both cases, experience had been considerably altered by instinct-laden fantasies. In that of hysteria, the relevant fantasies were erotic. The character of the early superego indicated that the fantasies that had entered into its formation were cruel and destructive.

Klein took this coloring of the infant's early experience of the parents as an expression of a tendency to project destructive fantasies and impulses to the outside world. Since the world of infancy, and particularly of early infancy, consists largely of the infant's parents, they are the inevitable objects of these projections. The projection of destructive impulses outward is found so regularly in infancy because it is a vital defense: As indicated in the previous chapter, infants experience their loving impulses as life-giving forces that are intimately connected to the preservation of their own lives. They likewise experience their hatred and destructive impulses as extremely dangerous threats to their own existence, which they must avoid at all costs. (We must recall that this stage of life is so dominated by concrete and magical thinking that ordinary adult symbolic speech and metaphor cannot convey the quality of its fantasy and thought. When considering this period, we must take phrases such as "bursting with anger" or "consumed with hatred, jealousy, or envy" more as concrete experiences than as figures of speech.) The equipment they have available for this task consists of their instinctual endowment toward projection and introjection, which is a manifestation of their innate oral and anal impulses. A substantial part of the infant's destructive impulses are projected to the outside, so that they are felt no longer to reside in the self but in an external object. Infants then experience their hatred and the danger that accompanies it as arising from their objects. This relieves them from the unbearable anxiety of being annihilated by forces inherent in the self, but places them in the (somewhat more tolerable) situation of feeling surrounded by dangerous, powerful, and hostile objects on the outside.

When these external parents are taken inside via introjection, they form the severe, primitive superego of infancy:

This apparently earliest measure of defense on the part of the ego [the projection of destructive impulses] constitutes, I think, the foundation-stone of the development of the super-ego. . . .

This view of the matter makes it also less puzzling to understand why the child should form such monstrous and phantastic images of his parents. For he perceives his anxiety arising from his aggressive instincts as a fear of his external object, both because he has made that object their outward goal, and because he has projected them onto it so they seem to be initiated against himself from that quarter. (The infant has, incidentally, some real grounds for fearing its mother, since it becomes growingly aware that she has the power to grant or withhold the gratification of its needs.) [1933, p. 250]

The net result is that the infant experiences its dangerous, destructive impulses no longer as linked to itself but as residing in persecutors, external and internal. Klein's theories about the early development of the superego enabled psychoanalysts to address earlier and more deeply unconscious foundations of neurosis in children and adults, with important clinical results.

Her theoretical conclusions have also radically altered our ideas of early psychological development. The highly destructive superego previously thought to be present only in certain seriously ill neurotics was now recognized as being present to some degrees at a very early point in everyone's development.[1] Klein does not suggest that infants are normally paranoid or ill, although in the older child or adult the states she describes would be classified clinically as such. She suggests that infants normally suffer from a kind of anxiety that in the adult or older child is prominent only during periods of psychosis. In this sense infants may be said to experience a psychotic type of anxiety, although not psychosis itself, as a part of normal development. This state of affairs is part of what Klein had in mind when she dismissed the bliss of infancy as a myth, and declared that

---

[1]The problem of moral masochism was now transformed: It was now not why some patients exhibited such a destructive superego, but how others had managed to develop a more benign one to the extent that they have. This problem is addressed in the next two chapters.

in reality an "immeasurable degree of suffering" is to be found in the earliest stages of childhood.

Klein's reliance on Freud's never-popular theory of an innate destructive force no doubt accounts for part of the opposition that her overall views have encountered even among psychoanalysts. Indeed, one gets the impression from her writings that she opposed it herself—that is, that she arrived at it quite reluctantly. But this unpalatable theory knitted together the clinical data better than any other available. Recognizing that uncongeniality is a poor argument against a theory, she accepted it.

Splitting and the Early Development of the Internal Object World

The superego is the prototype of what Klein called an *internal object*. Internal objects are formed by the two-stage process of projecting one's loving or hating impulses into an appropriate external object (thereby bringing it to psychological life), and then introjecting this object. The projection of hating and destructive impulses, which are equated with destructive parts of the self, into the frustrating object forms what Klein called a *bad object*. The bad object differs from a frustrating object by virtue of its having acquired intentionality: As a result of the projection of the infant's hatred and destructive impulses, the frustrating object is imbued with the psychological qualities of the hating part of the self. It becomes not simply frustrating, but destructive, hating, dangerous, and malevolent.

The projection of loving impulses into the *gratifying* external objects that occasion their arousal is felt to imbue the object with qualities of goodness, love, and concern, converting it from a reliever of tension into a psychologically meaningful *good object*.

But because these processes entail a great deal of splitting and separation of loving and destructive impulses (indeed, that is one of their vital defensive functions), objects at this point tend to be perceived as either all good or all bad. The frustrating object (for example, the mother's breast that is absent when hunger strikes the infant) is felt to be all bad, and completely separate from the gratifying object (the breast that relieves hunger), which is felt to be all good. Klein called such objects *part objects*, meaning that the infant perceived only part of the real object, the part that corresponds to the loving and hating impulses dominating the mind at the moment.

Vestiges of these early unconscious processes may be found outside the psychoanalytic playroom, in the myths and fairy tales that express our states of mind during the prehistoric epoch of splitting and projection. Young children accept the existence of a magical fairy godmother because they know from their own experiences that she is real: She corresponds to the "good" part-object of their inner worlds, an ideal mother who can gratify their needs virtually before they arise, and who furthermore has no other pressing business that would prevent her from doing so. The corresponding "bad" part-object, the mother who is absent when need arises, is represented as a very bad, omnipotently dangerous figure, the evil queens, witches, monsters, and ogres of fairy tales. At this point in the child's development, the bad object bears no more relation to the good one than an evil monster does to the benevolent godmother or kindly father.

The clear division between the armies of good and evil found in fairy tales expresses the world view that the small child had developed in infancy. Evil forces represent the child's destructive impulses and good ones represent loving impulses; their purity reflects the precision of the split in the infant minds between the loving and hating aspects of themselves. The disturbing tendency of good forces to transform themselves into evil ones in fairy tales corresponds to the tendency of the child's love to be replaced mercurially by hatred in the face of frustration. Note that in fairy tales it is not a question of a good figure having evil traits, or vice versa: Good figures are good and bad ones bad. The good figure who becomes bad turns out to have been a bad one all along, disguised as good. Thus is splitting proof against experience.

Splitting and projection together form the outward arc of a cycle of psychological metabolism. The inward arc is introjection, in which the external object (now experienced as containing the impulses or parts of the self that had previously been projected into it) is taken back in—in fantasy, swallowed—to form an internal object. Projection and introjection produce a psychological give-

and-take between the infant's inner world and environment. They act on one hand to endow the external world with psychological significance and on the other to modify and build up the inner world on the basis of experiences with the outer one.

The Paranoid–Schizoid Position

During the first months of life, moments of gratification give rise to feelings of unbridled bliss, based on fantasies of being fused and united with a good object. Moments of frustration summon up the specter of a malevolent and inescapable bad object, which creates severe and pervasive anxiety for the survival of oneself and one's good objects. The blissful state often alternates with the anxious one in a precipitous manner, a fact that corresponds to the transitory nature of an infant's moods. This polarization of the infant's world into an all good and an all bad part results from the highly active splitting processes that dominate this stage of life. The presence of the bad object produces an anxiety that in psychoanalytic terminology is called paranoid anxiety.

In recognition of the prevalence in it of splitting processes and of the character of the resultant anxiety, Klein called the state of mind that dominates this early phase of life the *paranoid–schizoid position*. She used the term *position* rather than *phase* or *stage* because she wanted to describe a specific unconscious constellation of anxieties, defenses, and relationships to objects that, although originating at or shortly after birth, persist throughout all stages of life, as the mental life of the infant within the adult, unconsciously influencing our world views and conscious states of mind.

Projective Identification

In 1946, Klein published her "Notes on Some Schizoid Mechanisms," a landmark paper in which she formulated the concept of *projective identification*. Projective identification is a crystallization of her ideas about the balance and interaction of projection and introjection in the formation and operation of the mind. Identification is the psychological consequence of introjection. When one takes an object inside oneself in fantasy, one feels that one has become somehow like it. Projection and identification, along with splitting, are unconscious fantasies that, due to their being experienced as concrete and real, have a real effect on the state and development of the mind. They form a part of psychic reality. With the term *projective identification*, Klein delineated a kind of identification in which the subject's experience of the nature of the object is significantly altered by the subject's projections into the object before or during the process of introjection. Her grasp of the phenomenon of projective identification showed how and why "psychic reality is of greater [or at least equal] importance than material reality" not only in neurosis, as Freud had recognized, but in all other unconscious operations of the mind as well. The immediate mover of the psyche is not external events, but our unconscious perception of them.

The way in which projective identification acts as the architect of unconscious psychic reality is shown by a dream that a college professor had in anticipation of her first meeting with her analyst. In her dream,

> the patient arrives at the analyst's office only to find that it has been transformed into a decorator's studio full of colorful fabrics, which the analyst had apparently created. She feels she is supposed to admire the fabrics and the analyst for designing them. She becomes mildly irritated by his increasingly flamboyant manner and by the fact that he has ignored her analysis, and expects her to "treat" him instead with her admiration.

The patient associated to the dream only a feeling of always having to be the one to look after others. But as the analysis progressed, she became increasingly aware of another feeling—which she could not account for—that she was supposed to admire and agree with the analyst's interpretations. Analysis of this feeling showed that it was connected to her wish to be admired by others, and to her assumption that others had the same wish.

The patient's perception of the analyst in the anticipatory dream as a demanding decorator could now be recognized as showing a deeper aspect of this same process. He was portrayed in that way as a consequence of her having projected onto him, during the formation of the dream, her own demand for admiration. She projected this demand because she felt unconsciously that she should not have it. When she disposed of her demand to be admired in a similar way during her sessions — by projective identification into the analyst — she felt herself unconsciously to have switched places with him: She now became the analyst, while the analyst became the disavowed part of herself, demanding approval and admiration. The result was that, although she consciously believed the analyst to be an analyst, she felt in her heart — that is, in psychic reality — that he was a kind of decorator whose fabric-interpretations she was obliged to treat with admiration, whether she wanted to or not. This unconscious perception of the analyst, her psychic reality molded by projection identification, was of greater importance than her conscious one in forming her emotional experience of the analysis.

Projective identification operates on two levels. The first is the level of unconscious fantasy that we have been considering. The second is also unconscious, but is "realistic." On this level, the subject acts in various ways to mold external reality so that it conforms better to what, in fantasy, had been projected into it. One of the earliest forms of projective identification depends on this realistic aspect as a means of communication: Infants who are attuned to their mothers quickly learn how to convey their own states of mind by realistically evoking a similar one in the mother. As a result, a receptive mother is able to intuit her baby's needs with remarkable speed and accuracy. This evocation of a state of mind in another for purposes of communication continues to be used throughout life, and many communications, especially artistic ones, owe much of their power and emotional resonance to projective identification.

The use to which projective identification is put depends on one's unconscious intent. Projective identification in its realistic aspect may be used not only for communication, but also for the control of another person through coercion or seduction. In this case, the underlying fantasy is one of aggressively planting an emotion — experienced as a concrete thing — inside an object, whereupon it is felt to take over and control the object. This fantasy is given reality by behavior that tends not only to produce a desired state of mind in another person, as in the communicative use of projective identification, but also to do so in a way from which they are not intended to be able to escape. The intent behind this type of projective identification is hostile, and in its earliest form it constitutes what Klein (1946) called the "prototype of an aggressive object-relation." Hypnosis and other forms of social, political, and therapeutic control owe much of their power to projective identification used in the service of seduction or coercion.

When used in this way, projective identification has an important consequence for the subject. He tends to experience the object as controlling him in return. One of the great difficulties in analyzing patients who use projective identification liberally in the service of controlling their objects is that they tend to experience words only as a subtle form of coercion. This makes it difficult to convince them that an interpretation is intended merely as food for thought, and is not the analyst's way of injecting into them something he is supposed to want them to feel.

Both the use of projective identification as a form of communication and as a means of controlling one's objects is shown in this vignette from the analysis of a 7-year-old boy who was brought to analysis because, among other symptoms, he was unable to accept even simple and reasonable direction from his parents.

For several sessions preceding the one to be described, he had insisted that the analyst act and speak only with his permission, and became increasingly anxious and frenetic in his efforts to control every detail of the play.

During this period, he constructed a toy "robot" whose command he assumed. The word "robot" was a play on the analyst's name, which indicated that the robot stood for the analyst. This was also shown by the fact that, when the analyst continued to speak without permission, the boy removed the robot's head. The decapitation meant that it was not even to think for itself. Upon seeing this, the analyst realized that, without being fully aware of it, he had indeed been feeling that he was not even to use his own head. The patient had managed to convey this constricting state of mind to him with great precision without either of them having put it into words.

The next day, the patient began his session by announcing that the playroom was a special school, where "bad children [a role assigned to the analyst] who did not listen" are sent to be "bossed around all day by the teachers" and not allowed to do anything on their own, not even to think or grow.

The analyst said that the boy was showing him how it felt to have parents inside him who wouldn't let him think for himself or grow up to be whoever he is. He listened to this with interest, and the analyst went on to say that when the boy turned the analyst and his parents into his robots, he felt they were inside him doing the same in return. With this interpretation, the boy appeared greatly relieved and began for the first time in weeks to play freely and spontaneously.

The "school" represented the boy's mind, and the bossy teachers the internal parents, his superego. His resistance to direction from his parents was connected to his extremely controlling superego: He took them as its external representatives. From his point of view he was fighting to keep them from turning him into a machine. The key to this perception of his parents is seen in the construction of the robot, which was a representation of the patient's fantasy that he could take over and control his objects by turning them into his robots. By actually placing the analyst in the position of a robot, he not only communicated to him how rigidly controlled he felt, but gave an aggressive reality to his fantasy of controlling the analyst. In the very strict special "school" he ran for his objects in his unconscious (and, through realistic projective identification, to some extent in reality as well), they were not allowed to have lives of their own, or even think for themselves. Following the interpretation of this fantasy, his parents reported that he became considerably less paranoid and more amenable to reason.

Projective Identification and the Psychoanalysis of Schizophrenia

Finally, there is the massive and aggressive type of projective identification characteristic of psychotic states. Until the elucidation of projective identification, the psychoanalytic approach to psychotic patients had been blocked at the outset by the extreme difficulty of making any analytic contact with them at all. Most analysts, starting with Freud, had considered them unable to form the kind of relationship with the analyst — the transference — that is necessary for analysis. Klein found that much of the analyst's difficulty in making contact with psychotic patients was due to the patient's employment of projective identification in a massive way. Withdrawn psychotic patients are dominated by the unconscious fantasy that they have so massively infiltrated the minds of their objects with parts of their own personalities that the object virtually has no longer any mind of its own, and needn't be regarded as a separate personality. In the transference, the analyst becomes another such object. The psychotic patient, therefore, appears not to relate to the analyst because he cannot unconsciously distinguish himself from the analyst. Massive projective identification, which made it appear that psychotic patients formed no relationship to the analyst, *was* the relationship to the analyst. The massiveness of their projections also contributes to the sense of depersonalization, or loss of contact with oneself, from which psychotic patients suffer.

Compounding the analyst's difficulty in coping with such a transference is the sense of mental paralysis that psychotic patients tend to induce in those around them. They do so partly in order to give some reality to the fantasy that their objects have no minds of their own, and partly as an expression of their destructive attacks on the analyst's ability to think and work. These attacks are the manifestation in the transference of the hostile and destructive impulses by which psychotic patients are dominated, and which they direct toward their objects in general. A good illustration of the sophistication that may be found in such attacks on the analyst's ability to think is given by Bion in his report (1954) of a patient who began a session by saying "I think the sessions are not for a long while but stop me ever going out." Then, while the analyst was still paralyzed by the effort to comprehend this, he asked with genuine innocence how the elevator knows what to do when he pushes two buttons at once.

These attacks on the analyst's thinking are paralleled by similar attacks made by the destructive, psychotic part of the schizophrenic's personality on his own ability to think. The analyst's understanding of projective identification and his experiencing its effect on himself gives him an insight into similar processes occurring within the patient—or rather, shows him precisely what it feels like to be schizophrenic. The patient's internal attacks contribute to the disorders of thinking from which schizophrenics suffer. In this sense, the schizophrenic's attack on the analyst's thinking may also serve to communicate to the analyst something of the patient's own state of mind.

Klein found that the massive and destructive use of projective identification by schizophrenic patients may be diminished if one interprets it rigorously, consistently, and in detail. Once the use of projective identification is thoroughly and accurately interpreted, patients become more available for further analysis along more conventional lines. A number of Klein's students have attempted to psychoanalyze schizophrenic patients from the perspective provided by her work on projective identification. They confined themselves to interpreting the unconscious, including the patient's unconscious use of massive projective identification, avoiding, as one would with a neurotic patient, suggestion, drugs, reassurance, or other non-analytic measures aimed at suppressing symptoms. These analyses placed severe technical demands on the analyst, and could be conducted only under highly favorable external circumstances.

They reported their attempts in a series of papers published during the late 1940s and 1950s (Rosenfeld 1947, 1950, 1952a, 1952b, 1954; Segal 1950, 1956; Bion 1954, 1956, 1957, 1959). They found that analysis conducted along these lines increased their patients' ability to make contact with themselves and with the analyst as well. Such alterations are not the same as those associated with spontaneous remissions, which produce symptomatic improvement without any change in underlying psychological structures. They were, rather, structural alterations of the patient's personality, which consisted of integration of the various parts of the patient's ego on an unconscious level. Following these developments, analysis of such patients along more conventional lines became possible for the first time. The achievement of this kind of integration indicates that psychoanalysis had indeed taken place in patients previously considered unanalyzable. This has pointed a direction for future psychoanalytic research into the psychological roots of schizophrenia.

16

The Transformation of the Superego: Psychological Integration and Growth

Klein's analyses of children revealed that, in addition to the relatively mature superego that produced realistic guilt and appeared to emerge at the resolution of the Oedipus complex, there was another, more primitive superego that arose in the first year of life, and it produced not guilt but terrifying anxieties. Normally, the primitive superego evolves into the more mature form as part of psychological development. In neurosis, however, it remained a dominant psychological force even into adulthood.

Klein was unable for many years to answer the two questions posed by this discovery: How did this impressive transformation occur in the course of normal development, and what blocked its occurrence in neurosis? She eventually found the answer more or less serendipitously during her reevaluation of Freud's work on the problem of depressive illness. In the 20 years that had elapsed since Freud had shown that melancholia was connected to an identification with a lost object, her work on splitting, projection, and

introjection had shed a great deal of light on the processes underlying identification. Armed with these insights, she was able to reach
more deeply and probe more precisely than Freud had into the
underpinnings of depression.

She began her reexamination by recounting her findings about
the early stages of normal development, when the infant's ego is
confronted with a split-up world of ideally good and ideally bad
objects, both external and internal. Experiences with good external
objects, in conjunction with the infant's loving impulses, promote
the formation of good internal ones. This in turn gives the infant the
feeling of being filled with good things that constitutes the unconscious basis of internal well-being and security. Once good internal
objects are established, they begin to nurture and strengthen the
ego. The stronger ego is emboldened to slowly relinquish the
splitting and projection to which it had hitherto to resort as a defense
against the danger of its destructive impulses. As a result, good and
bad objects, both external and internal, begin to lose their extremely
polar character and come gradually to resemble each other more
closely in the infant's mind. Eventually, the infant becomes aware
that its good object, for example the gratifying mother toward whom
its loving impulses are directed, and its bad object, the frustrating
mother that is the target of its destructive impulses, are one and the
same person. This means that the infant now finds itself in a
relationship not with idealized objects but with objects that are a
mixture of loved and hated qualities.

Recalling that the formation of ideally good and bad objects is
the result of a defensive split in the self, we can see that this decrease
in splitting of the object is a sign of a decrease in splitting of the self.
This means that the infant now begins to have a more integrated and
realistic experience of itself. It feels for the first time that hostile and
malevolent forces arise not only from a bad object, directed toward
the self, but also arise from itself, directed at objects. The net effect
of diminished splitting is that the infant begins to experience both
itself and its objects no longer as idealized repositories of good or
evil, but as something more like people, mixtures of good and bad.
Since both the object and the self are no longer experienced so much
as good or bad fragments, but as two separate, whole, and complex

individuals, the infant is now said to have a relation with a "whole object." Parents are often aware of the effects of this unconscious development when they describe the baby's "becoming a person" at around 4 to 6 months of age.

This decisive change in the infant's relationship to its objects produces a fundamental change in the nature of its predominant anxieties. Previously, the infant was capable only of conceiving anxiety due to threats to its own survival emanating from bad objects. With the recognition that the loved and hated objects are identical, the infant begins to feel a new anxiety on behalf of the loved object as well, now felt to be exposed to very real danger from destructive parts of the self. At this point, the infant becomes aware of its own inability to protect its good object from the destructive impulses that arise within it in response to inevitable frustrations. The infant is then confronted with a dilemma that, in Klein's words, precipitates intense "guilt and remorse . . . a sense of responsibility for preserving [the good object] intact against persecutors and the id, and . . . sadness relating to expectations of the impending loss of it." (1935, p. 270).

This state of affairs forms the prototype—the unconscious basis—for grief and mourning later in life. When an adult or child grieves,

> in the last analysis it is the ego's unconscious knowledge that the hate is indeed also there, as well as the love, and that it may at any time get the upper hand (the ego's anxiety of being carried away by the id and so destroying the loved object), which brings about the sorrow, feelings of guilt and the despair which underlie grief. [1935, pp. 270–271]

A period of grieving, guilt, and remorse therefore forms part of every infant's development. These painful emotions are psychologically justified, since the damage done to the loved object by the infant's hatred has psychic reality. However difficult to bear, they nevertheless form an extremely important part of the infant's development. They are, Klein wrote, "whether conscious or unconscious . . . in my view among the essential and fundamental elements of the feelings we call love" (1935, p. 270).

This means that

> the child's development depends on, and to a large extent is
> formed by, his capacity to find the way to bear inevitable and
> necessary frustrations and the conflicts of love and hate which
> are in part caused by them: that is, to find a way between his
> hate which is increased by frustrations, and his love and wish for
> reparation which bring in their train the sufferings of remorse.
> The way the child adapts himself to these problems in his mind
> forms the foundation for all his later social relationships, his
> adult capacity for love and cultural development. He can be
> immensely helped in childhood by the love and understanding of
> those around him, but these deep problems can neither be solved
> for him nor abolished. [1937, p. 316n]

Klein called the infant's state of mind during this period the *depressive
position*. Despite its name, the infantile depressive position is not the
prototype of depressive illness, but rather of the capacity for love
and concern, and its corollaries, mourning and grief.[1]

The suffering the infant endures in the depressive position as a
result of the integration of its love and hatred differs from the
anxieties of the paranoid-schizoid position in two important re-
spects: It is felt on behalf of a loved object rather than for the self
alone, and—because it is based on love and remorse—it consists of
mental pain and anguish rather than terror. The two types of
anxiety

> can be distinguished from one another if, as a criterion of
> differentiation, one considers whether the . . . anxiety is mainly
> related to the preservation of the ego—in which case it is
> paranoic—or the preservation of the good internalized objects
> with which the ego is identified as a whole. In the latter case—
> which is the case of the depressive—the anxiety and feelings of
> suffering are of a much more complex nature. The anxiety lest
> the good object and with them the ego should be destroyed, or
> that they are in a state of disintegration, is interwoven with

---

[1]The relationship between the depressive position and depressive illness will be
taken up later in this chapter.

continuous and desperate efforts to save the good objects both internalized and external. [1935, p. 269]

Klein called this complex distress *depressive anxiety* to distinguish it from the persecutory anxiety of the paranoid-schizoid position.

The discovery of the depressive position and its attendant anxieties provided the answer to the question of how the mature superego normally replaced the more primitive one. The extreme splitting that characterizes the paranoid-schizoid position creates fantastically idealized part-objects, both good and bad. The primitive superego is the result of the introjection of such objects, and is therefore a mixture of ideally good and bad part-objects. But in the paranoid-schizoid position, even the relationship with the ideally good part-object is fraught with anxiety, since, when the infant makes such great demands on an idealized good object — as, for instance, that it be inexhaustible and ever-present — the object is experienced as making similar demands on the infant in return, and becomes in its own way a persecutor. Furthermore, the relationship with the good part-object contains neither gratitude nor concern. Since an ideally good part-object is felt to be inexhaustible, one doesn't feel that what one has received from it has cost it anything, which means that no gratitude is felt. Likewise, since it is invulnerable, one doesn't feel that anything that one does to it will harm it, which means that it need not be treated with respect or concern.

The mature superego, on the other hand, is an internal object formed by an identification with a parent who is experienced more as a whole object. One feels gratitude, love, and concern for a whole object that is not felt toward an idealized one because the whole object is felt to be limited, vulnerable and human, not god- or demonlike. Love and concern for a parent entails the guilt, remorse, and anxiety about one's ability to preserve it in the face of one's hatred, which distinguishes the depressive position, and only by facing both the love and hatred felt for the parents, and finding a way between the two emotions, can the child achieve a real loving relationship with them.

When the child is able to experience concern for the internalized parents that form the superego, the child feels that they are concerned for the self in return. The superego of the depressive position mirrors the ego's desire not just to attack the frustrating ("bad") mother, but to preserve her out of an awareness that she is also good. The superego is therefore felt to want not merely to attack the self for being bad, but to help it and preserve it. The transformation of the superego from its primitive to its mature form is part of the developmental transition from the paranoid-schizoid to the depressive position.

Injuries done in psychic reality to a good (whole) internal object are not felt to create a persecuting bad object, but an injured good one. The intrapsychic result is the feelings of sorrow, guilt, and remorse that Klein described as part of the depressive position. These emotions, while painful, are not as unbearable as the persecution that issues from the primitive, retaliating superego. Moreover, injuries to an internal object for whom one feels concern are felt to be potentially reparable — the concern itself seems to make them so — and this gives rise in the depressive position to a real hope and optimism about the inner and outer worlds that is absent in the paranoid–schizoid position.

The ease and success with which the transition from the paranoid-schizoid to the depressive position is made depends to some extent on the degree of splitting and projective identification to which the infant had to resort earlier during the paranoid-schizoid position. Excessive splitting and projection of destructive impulses produces many very bad objects, both external and internal, which leads to extreme persecutory anxiety, which leads in turn to more splitting and projection to rid oneself of the bad objects, and so on in a vicious cycle.

Counteracting these effects is the developmental logic of the forces of integration: Any success in integration brings relief from the anxieties of the paranoid–schizoid position and encourages further integration.

> When the infant reaches the depressive position, and becomes more able to face his psychic reality, he also feels that the object's badness is largely due to his own aggressiveness and the ensuing projection. This insight, as we can see in the transference situation, gives rise to great mental pain and guilt when the depressive position is at its height. But it also brings about

feelings of relief and hope, which in turn make it less difficult to reunite the two aspects of the object and of the self and to work through the depressive position. This hope is based on the growing unconscious knowledge that the internal and external object is not as bad as it was felt to be in its split-off aspects. Through mitigation of hatred by love the object improves in the infant's mind. It is no longer so strongly felt to have been destroyed in the past and the danger of its being destroyed in the future is lessened; not being injured, it is also felt to be less vulnerable in the present and future. [Klein 1957, p. 196]

This leads away from the vicious cycle of splitting and persecutory anxiety, and into a positive developmental spiral. Klein's phrase "mitigation of hatred by love" captures the emotional meaning of the technical term *psychological integration*. The painful bringing together of loving and hating feelings for the same object diminishes the strength of one's hatred for it, which then makes the object seem not as damaged, malevolent, and persecuting as it had before. This in turn gives rise to renewed hope and optimism for oneself: One's psychic reality (that is, one's experience of the internal object world) seems not as bad as before, and the possibilities of facing and improving it seem more real. The repeated experience that one's internal objects have survived one's hatred contributes to a psychologically justified feeling of inner resilience. Klein suggests that the repeated experience of the good object's surviving one's hatred of it is not only conducive to psychological growth, but is a necessary part of it. "When these negative states are transient, the good object is regained time and time again. This is an essential factor in establishing it and in laying the foundations of stability and a strong ego." [1957, p. 187]

The Depressive Position and the Sense of Reality

In the paranoid–schizoid position, the predominant mode of identification is projective identification. Because it is based on an unconscious fantasy that a part of one has invaded the object, it does not cause one to identify with an object in the sense of becoming *like*

192 Melanie Klein's Development of Freud's Work

it, but rather causes one to feel that one somehow *is* it. The fusion between the good parts of the self and the good object, and between the bad parts of the self and the bad object, that occurs as a result of projective identification produces in its most primitive form a state of mind that amounts to complete confusion between self and object. As splitting and projection become less extreme, the character of projective identification tends to moderate. Gradually, the object is recognized more and more as separate from oneself, although perhaps still seen as having some of one's attributes.

As splitting and projection diminish still more, and as the distinction between self and object consequently becomes even more complete, a sense of reality—that is, the ability to distinguish internal from external reality—begins to supervene. With this development, another type of identification, which Klein called *introjective identification*, becomes possible. As projective identification is associated with the splitting processes of the paranoid–schizoid position, introjective identification is connected to the integration of the depressive position. It is based on a relationship with a whole object, whose separate existence is recognized even as it is identified with. Introjective identification produces not the feeling that one is indeed the loved object, but a feeling that one can be somehow *like* it. It is associated with the striving to be like a loved and admired ideal, which must always fall short. Introjective identification creates an intrapsychic climate quite different from that which results from projective identification. The control of the object inherent in projective identification produces an internal object that is felt to reciprocate by controlling one from within. But the recognition, inherent in introjective identification, that the object has a life of its own produces an identification with an object that allows one an internal life of one's own, and so promotes the growth of an independent ego.[2]

The unconscious capacity to make the distinction between self

---

[2]This point is conveyed in William Blake's lines:
He who bends to himself a joy
Does the winged life destroy;
But he who kisses the joy as it flies
Lives in eternity's sunrise.

and object results from the distinguishing of self from nonself that forms part of the integrative processes of the depressive position. When we speak of someone being in contact with reality, we mean precisely that he or she is able to distinguish the outer world from the inner one, external reality from psychic reality. Since the capacity to perceive external reality accurately and the capacity to perceive psychic reality accurately are formed at the same time, the results of a single process, a defect in one's awareness of one's psychic reality implies a defect in one's perception of external reality as well.

Reparation

The decrease in the infant's splitting of self and objects allows it to perceive its objects in a more realistic way. This has the twofold effect of making it aware that it is separate from its objects and of increasing its sense of the good object's value for it. One result of this is a growing sense both of the need the infant feels for the good object, and of its value. This gives rise to the urge to care for and preserve the good object, and to undo the damage the infant feels it has already done to it. In technical terms, depressive pain leads to reparative urges. Because these urges are based on love for the good object, they are felt to preserve and restore it. The newly restored good internal object in turn further strengthens and restores the ego. This assists the ego to integrate itself and its objects still further.

The acknowledgment of one's own destructive impulses, which forms the essential first step of reparation, means that unlike splitting and projection, reparation is not a defense against psychic pain but a way of working it through. The crucial difference between reparation and psychological defenses is that the latter, although at times necessary for psychological survival, do not lead to psychological growth, while reparation does precisely that. As Segal (1981) expresses it:

> Reparation . . . arises out of feeling of loss and guilt experienced in the depressive position. Reparation is based on love for the object and the wish to restore it and regain it. The reparative drives contribute to the development of the ego and the object

relationships; they cannot be considered a defense since reparation does not aim at denying psychic reality, but is an endeavor — realistic in psychic terms — to resolve depressive anxiety and guilt. [p. 147]

Manic Defenses and Depressive Illness

The pain and remorse that are inextricably bound to reparation give rise to new defenses, aimed at avoiding them. These *manic defenses*, as Klein called them, consist of a revival of splitting and projection that attacks the sources of depressive pain on all fronts. They diminish the sense of the goodness and value of the good (whole) object that the child has gained through its entry into the depressive position, which reduces the love the child feels for it, which in turn makes the damage that the child unconsciously feels he has done to it seem less important. The manic defense leads to a devaluation of the loved object, followed by an idealization of other objects of lesser importance, to which the child then turns. In turning away from the loved object, the child acquires a sense of triumph at having been freed from the good object, which, in addition to being loved, is also hated for causing the depressive pain. The devaluation of the good object is felt in the unconscious to damage it, but remorse over this state of affairs, which might lead to repair of the situation, cannot be experienced, since the psychic pain that would be involved is precisely what is being defended against. The state of mind created by the manic defense therefore tends to persist for many years, continually undermining love for the primal good objects of infancy.

Since it is this love, kept alive in the unconscious, that forms the basis of love for all other objects, undermining it affects the capacity to love everyone and everything else. In extreme cases, these feelings may lead to the grandiosity, omnipotence, and narcissism of clinical mania. But even in milder cases, manic defenses tend to make the subject's world empty, and to leave the personality shallow, aimless, and impoverished.

Another important clinical consequence of the manic defense is depressive illness. Its symptoms are themselves primarily manifestations of the manic attack on the good object (a turning away from it, reflected clinically in a turning away from the world and loss of appetite for various things in life), of the subsequent identification with it in its damaged state (which produces the symptoms of a sense of worthlessness and lifelessness), and of the resultant persecution by it (the symptoms of agitation, sleeplessness, and inability to concentrate). The fact that manic illness and depressive illness may arise from a common cause—the unconscious manic defense—explains their tendency to be found alternating with each other in manic-depressive (bipolar) illness.

There is a special form of manic defense that represents a middle area between ordinary manic defenses and reparation. Klein called this special form *manic reparation*. This is an attempt to magically repair the damaged object without experiencing the grief and remorse stemming from the damage that one feels one has done to it in the unconscious. Manic reparation is ineffective precisely because it circumvents the painful awareness of the effects of one's hatred toward the loved object, which itself constitutes the central work of reparation. Forms of psychotherapy that focus on suppressing guilt and anxiety are based on manic reparation. Segal (1981) distinguishes between true reparation and manic reparation in this way: "Manic trends in reparation . . . aim at denying guilt, and are based on omnipotent control of the object. The defense against anxiety and guilt is paramount and love and concern for the object—the hallmark of genuine reparation—are relatively weak" (p. 147).

The painful difficulty of achieving integration and the constant liability to renewed splitting and manic defenses that undo it are illustrated in the following vignette, taken from the analysis of a housewife in her late 20s who entered analysis because of her fear of having a child. She also suffered from an inability to identify what she felt, which was connected to a fear that she would express excessive hostility or be too "nosy."

She reported a dream several days before Thanksgiving in which

> she saw three or four pairs of animals in a box. They were shriveled up, and she felt she had neglected them. One pair were rats, and another hamsters. She thought she could save the

hamsters by sprinkling water on them. When she did this, they "fluffed up" like sponges. To her horror, the rats were also revived. She kept the hamsters and threw the rats away.

She associated the hamsters to a hamster once owned by an adolescent niece who was visiting her at the time of the dream. The hamster had died and the patient recalled the niece feeling somehow responsible, as though she had starved it. She went on to say, with considerable emotion, that her niece had been an unappreciative houseguest and had actually responded spitefully to the patient's attempts to entertain her. She then said that rats were "horrible, invasive" things. The analyst interpreted the animals as the patient's feelings, the hamsters her genuine positive feelings (as distinct from a facade of good feeling she wore to mask her true feelings), and the rats her hostility and invasive "nosiness." The animals were dried out because she had stifled them, out of fear of the rats. When her feelings, both good and bad, were awakened in the analysis, she needed to throw the bad rat-feelings away—project them into her niece, which sharpens her awareness of the niece's hostility and spitefulness while blinding her to her own. The analyst added that the rats seemed specifically to represent a spiteful denial of gratitude, which she felt she must get rid of because it would destroy her good hamster-feelings, which consisted in part of gratitude for the various things her life had to offer her.

The following day she began her session by saying that she was planning a Thanksgiving dinner, but dreaded it because she didn't know what to do about her disturbed sister-in-law. She said that she could stand the sister-in-law well enough herself, but knew her mother would be upset and enraged at having to eat with her. She wondered if there wasn't some way of excluding her sister-in-law from the gathering. It wouldn't be fair, she thought, to invite her mother and then spring someone like her sister-in-law on her. The analyst said that her rat-feelings had now been thrown away into her sister-in-law, who now represented them, and that her mother stood for the part of her that was enraged at having to discover them in her analysis. She was suggesting that it was unfair of the analyst to invite her into analysis and then face her with her upsetting feelings. The patient responded vehemently that she *couldn't* invite the two together, and said the analyst was putting her down and failing to appreciate the difficulty of her dilemma.

The analyst pointed out that she had taken his remark

about her intrapsychic dilemma as though he was talking about her family problem. She had pushed these aspects of herself into the members of her family so vigorously that it was now possible for her to conceive of them only as pertaining to the outside world. The patient then recognized with real emotion how enraged she was at having to face such feelings in herself, and her mood changed from a persecuted one to a more sober state.

She began the following session by reporting a dream in which she was gathering her whole family to thank two people who had helped them. She was awakened from this dream by her husband, who wanted her to quiet their noisy niece. Her attitude toward her niece had now softened; instead of resentment and hatred, she felt some concern for her. But her husband felt she had become "overinvolved" with the niece, and wanted her to "get tough." The analyst interpreted that her gathering the whole family represented an attempt at integration of the various parts of herself, and that the intent of thanking someone represents a feeling of gratitude to the analyst for the work that has promoted her integration. This was interfered with by the part of her that was enraged at the integration, this time projected into her husband ("her husband woke her up"), which wanted to get tough and simply shut up (restifle) her rat-feelings, which it again projected into her niece.

The following day, she reported spending a sleepless night. She seemed confused in the session, had no associations, and was quite difficult to make contact with. She made reference to her niece's and sister-in-law's ingratitude, and felt vaguely angry with them. The analyst said that the part of her that was enraged by the integration of the previous day attacked and splintered her ability to think in retaliation for the role her analytic thinking had in bringing about the integration. This left her in a disintegrated state. She then began to speak wistfully of a friend who, although quite disturbed in many ways, is still able to acknowledge her flaws. The patient clearly admired her friend's candor and honesty, which she felt was courageous, and which represented the integration that the patient longed for.

The following day she said she felt more "lively," but didn't know why. Perhaps it was because her niece was no longer "on strike," and had agreed to help her with the dishes. She felt more solid as well, but couldn't imagine the reason for that either. The analyst said that her feelings of liveliness and solidity might be related to the revival of her feelings, both hamster and rat, and to the integration that had accompanied it. This was connected to the analytic work of the previous several sessions, which she seemed at the time to have felt was quite important. The patient then realized that her puzzlement over her present state of mind was a denial of the help she had received from the analysis. She went on to say that the analyst's work now struck her as quite original—not "prepackaged" or the parroting of someone else's ideas. She added that she now felt for the first time like cooking a Thanksgiving dinner. This recognition of the value of the analyst's original work represented a mitigation of the rat part of her, which had been devaluing the analysis, by its integration with the loving hamster part. She could now identify with a creative analyst by being a cook whose work seemed to her to have some value.

In addition to representing her positive feelings, the fluffy hamsters also represented her good part-object, her mother's fluffy breasts. The rats represented her destructive feelings, primarily envy and sadism, that invaded and undermined her feelings of gratitude. When projected into her objects, they played a role in forming the bad, persecuting part-object. This identity of the good and bad part-objects with good and bad parts of the self is due to the inextricability of the part-object from parts of the self in the paranoid-schizoid position, to which the splitting and projection of the manic defense had temporarily returned the patient.

She attempted to deal with the rat-feelings and corresponding rat-objects by stifling all her feelings—by starving the animals. In the dream, she could not revive the hamsters without also inadvertantly reviving the rats. This represented the fact that she could not have positive feelings toward her loved object without these feelings also giving rise to hatred and envy of it, precisely because it is loved and admirable. Splitting and stifling contributed greatly to one of her major symptoms, her loss of contact with her feelings and her not knowing what she really felt. In addition, her tendency to project feared aspects of herself into her objects had made her afraid, in her unconscious, that if she had a baby of her own it would be a rat-baby, an anxiety that played a major role in her fear of having children.

Because the patient often projected good and bad parts of

herself into her external objects, especially the members of her family, they came in her unconscious to represent various parts of her. (This tendency, incidentally, also left her overly dependent on them in reality.) The dream in which she gathers her whole family represents an attempt at integration of these various parts, and her disintegrated state on the following day was a reaction against the integration expressed in the dream, and acted as a defense against the depressive pain contained in it.

In the last session, she attempted first to attribute her sense of well-being to factors extrinsic to the analysis. This was another attempt to deflect the pain connected with having to depend on the analyst, representing the good (whole) object in the transference, for her well-being. Her newly acquired liveliness was due to her having successfully integrated (acknowledged) some of her envy and resentment of the good object, which meant that they were now mitigated by her love for it. This brought it to life in her mind and produced in her the feeling of inner liveliness. The feeling of solidity, the conscious manifestation of an unconscious sense of no longer being split into scattered pieces, was a result of the same process.

Reparation, Creativity, and Normal Psychological Development

Klein's discovery that the superego of the normal adult develops out of a primitive one, present in all children and closely resembling the superegos of neurotic (and psychotic) patients, gave rise to the two questions, formulated at the beginning of this chapter, of how the transformation occurred (if it did) or what prevented it from occurring (if it didn't). They were answered in terms of the paranoid–schizoid and depressive positions. The transformation of the superego was part of a momentous transition from the paranoid–schizoid to the depressive position. This transition has its inception within the first six months of life, when psychological integration first occurs, but, never a fait accompli, continues throughout life in the form of psychological development.

Normal psychological development depends first on the adequate resolution of persecutory anxieties, which brings about integration, and next on the resolution of the depressive anxiety and guilt that result from it. The ego bears and resolves the guilt, remorse, and anxieties of the depressive position by making reparation in the unconscious to the good object that it feels it has damaged with its destructive impulses.

Among the ego's most effective forms of reparation are its creative impulses, represented by creative work. The term *creative work* must be taken here in the broadest sense (Jaques 1970). It includes not only works of art, but scientific endeavors, childrearing, meaningful labor of all kinds, cultural achievements such as the acquisition of language, all forms of learning, and creative play. Unconsciously, creative work is felt to flow from one's good, internal parents. The ability to perform it means that the good parents are alive and safe in the internal world, and that one's loving impulses have, therefore, at least temporarily overcome one's destructive impulses. The unconscious awareness of this contributes to the great reassurance and sense of inner well-being that creative work brings. Creative work may also be felt unconsciously to *undo* prior damage caused by one's hatred of the good object. Segal (1952, 1974) has described how the forms taken by one's creative work reflect in detail specific reparative urges and fantasies, tailored to undo the precise damage felt to have been done in fantasy to the internal object. The opportunity for creative work is therefore not a luxury, but a psychological necessity, and its absence exposes one to the risk of serious psychological illness. Jaques (1970) has outlined the vital implications of this fact for social and industrial policy.

17

The Early Stages of the
Oedipus Complex

F reud's model of the Oedipus complex, which he first proposed in 1900, was a reconstruction based on the data he obtained from his analyses of adults. It has withstood the test of time, at least in broad outline, so well that the impassioned controversy that greeted his first expression of it — and of the closely related issue of childhood sexuality — seems almost incomprehensible today. His reconstruction of the earlier psychological events of childhood out of which the Oedipus complex itself emerges was, however, hampered by the great distance from which he had to view them in his analyses of adults.

The technique of child psychoanalysis enabled Klein to fill in many details left out of Freud's model of oedipal development, and to reconstruct the prehistory of the Freudian Oedipus complex. This accumulation of new information about the early and later stages of the Oedipus complex led her to extend, supplement, and finally to recast Freud's original formulation.

In Freud's model, the boy comes under the influence of a strong wave of genital libido cresting at age 4 or 5, which causes him to develop a desire for sexual intercourse with his mother, to whom he has always been attached in various ways and for various reasons. But he soon becomes convinced that to pursue this course would lead to castration at the hands of his father. This causes him to abandon his sexual desire for her. In order to make this renunciation possible, he identifies with his father, thus effecting the simultaneous dissolution of the Oedipus complex and institution of the superego.

The girl's Oedipus complex (Freud 1933) is set in motion at about the same age as the boy's, when she first notices that she lacks a penis. This causes her to envy boys and men theirs, and to hold her mother responsible for her having formed her without one. In her resentment over this narcissistic wound, she turns away from her mother, who prior to this time had meant everything to her. In addition, to quell her envy of her father's penis, she turns toward him with the aim of acquiring it for herself. She soon realizes that this is impossible, and resigns herself to accepting a baby from him as the most satisfying substitute. This decision determines her ultimate sexual orientation.

A number of conclusions emerge from this picture. First, the boy abandons his oedipal wishes toward his mother in order to avoid castration, and the girl enters into the oedipal relationship with her father because, in her view, she already is castrated. Second, the boy resolves his oedipal conflict by identifying with his father, an event that Freud believed led to the formation of the superego, but the girl turns to the father primarily as an external object. She never *internalizes* either parent, and because of this, never *resolves* her Oedipus complex. She therefore never acquires the kind of solid superego, or the true independence from her parents, that the boy does when he internalizes his father. On this theory, women, compared to men, would be expected to have a weaker sense of justice, weaker social ties, and more dependence on other people (as substitutes for their never-internalized parents), and to be less courageous in their convictions. Freud was aware of the inadequacy of this model of female sexual development when he called it the weakest part of his psychology. But he was unable to improve on it, perhaps because, not being in a position to form any convictions about the details of phenomena that occur before the age of 4 or 5, he was unable to support a reasonable alternative.

Klein's direct investigations into the young child's psychological development showed that the Oedipus complex as described by Freud was a developmental consequence of earlier phenomena whose roots extend back into the first year of life: concrete unconscious fantasy, projection and introjection, splitting, and persecutory and depressive anxieties. When the ways in which these factors interact with and build upon one another are taken into account, a picture of oedipal development emerges that is strikingly similar for both sexes, and far more vivid and detailed than Freud's earlier approximations.

In this expanded view,

> the Oedipus complex starts during the first year of life and in both sexes begins to develop along similar lines. The relation to the mother's breast is one of the essential factors which determine the whole emotional and sexual development. I therefore take the breast relation as my starting point in the following description of the beginnings of the Oedipus complex in both sexes. [Klein 1945, pp. 407–408]

Starting at this point required her to explain what would motivate an infant attached to the mother's breast to widen its sphere of interest to include a second object, the father. She identified two forces that tend to bring this about. The first is the gratification that the infant experiences at the breast. This produces in the infant's mind a feeling of a "good" breast that leads it to expect a similar experience with other objects. On the basis of this expectation, the infant now turns its desire to new objects, starting with the father.

The second force that promotes interest in the father is, paradoxically, the opposite of the first:

> Particular emphasis, however, is given to the new desire [for the father] by frustration in the breast relation. It is important to remember that frustration depends on internal factors as well as on actual experiences. Some measure of frustration is inevitable, even under the most favorable circumstances, for what the infant actually desires is *unlimited* gratification. [1945, p. 408]

The infant forms an attachment to its father—the first step away from the breast into the wider world—because of an optimal combination of gratification and frustration at the breast. Too little gratification makes it difficult for the infant to form a positive attachment to the primal object, and thereby deprives it of its template for further positive attachments. Too much gratification (or even the attempt to provide it) deprives it of an important impetus to seek out new objects. Love for the breast combines with frustration at it to stimulate in both sexes the desire for an alternative.

In this frame of mind, the infant boy or girl turns toward the father with the wishful expectation that he will be an improvement over the breast. The infant's first rudimentary concept of its father is based partly on its experiences at the breast, and partly on hallucinatory gratification of its wish for an object that will anticipate and meet all its oral needs. The father is therefore seen, on the model of the breast, as an alternative object of oral gratification. The relationship to the father is still a part–object one, and the infant sees him as something like a nipple on which it may suck. This prototype forms the infant's primal concept of the penis.

The psychological discovery of the father's penis does not entirely avoid problems triggered by frustration at the breast. When it too proves incapable of offering unlimited gratification, the conflicting attitudes toward the breast, associated with a good and bad part–object breast, are carried over into the new relationship with the father's penis. Each of its two objects (breast and penis) is still split, and therefore liable in turn to become at times extremely good and at times extremely bad. The infant now has two idealized objects and two highly persecuting ones.

The infant has, however, accomplished something of value by including the father: A broader repertoire of objects has been created from which to select an ideally good and an ideally bad one. It can now move "to and fro between the various [good and bad] aspects" of two primary objects. Two objects—two parents—provide a reality that lends itself to splitting more readily than was the case with only one object. The infant may now direct its love toward one parent and its hatred toward the other. By widening its field of objects, the infant has increased its chances of successful splitting, on which its relative stability in the paranoid-schizoid position depends.

The Oedipus complex in its early stage is identical for both sexes because at this stage it serves a need that is the same in both sexes, the need to split. To each positive oedipal relationship with an ideally good object (breast or penis) corresponds a negative relationship with a terrifying bad object (penis or breast) that occupies the other side of the split. The need to secure the presence of an ideally good object while avoiding a very bad one causes the infant to direct its love, with equal likelihood and facility, alternately toward one parent and then toward the other. This brings into being, simultaneously and with the same force, a heterosexual Oedipus complex and a homosexual one. Each, serving the requirements of splitting equally well, is interchangeable with the other.

Moreover, even at this early, part–object stage, the parents are felt by the infant to have a relationship with each other. When loving feelings predominate in its mind, the infant has a sense of two good parents combining with each other to produce good things for one another and for the infant, and to help it cope with frustrations and dangerous, destructive impulses. When feelings of frustration dominate, however, the infant feels that its parents are giving all the milk and other good things to each other, while maliciously depriving the infant of them. When destructive impulses predominate, the infant may feel that its parents have become two very bad objects, attacking, poisoning and destroying each other. These various parental imagos fluctuate with each other in the infant's mind, and each parent is experienced at various times as extremely good or bad, isolated or in various kinds of combination with the other. The prevailing imago depends on the type of emotion that has gripped the infant at the moment.

From the beginning of life, the infant has a powerful oral tendency to "swallow" both parents in its fantasy, an event that produces a "double" of them (or rather its perception of them) in the internal infant world, thereby beginning the formation of the superego. The superego therefore emerges not at the dissolution of the Oedipus complex but at its very inception.

The imagos of his mother's breast and of his father's penis are established within [the infant's] ego to form the nucleus of his super-ego. To the introjection of the good and bad breast and mother corresponds the introjection of the good and bad penis and father. They become the first representatives on the one hand of protective and helpful figures, on the other of retaliating and persecuting internal figures, and are the first identifications which the ego develops. [1945, p. 409]

Up to this point, Klein has been describing oedipal phenomena related to the infant's need to split its world. But an opposing dynamic, related to the forces of integration, has also been active from the beginning in the development of the Oedipus complex. It is against the background of this force toward integration that genital impulses and fantasies make their first appearance.

Though still overshadowed by oral, urethral and anal libido, genital desires soon mingle with the child's oral impulses. Early genital desires, as well as oral ones, are directed towards mother and father. . . . In the male infant, genital sensations . . . imply a search for an opening into which to insert his penis, i.e. they are directed toward his mother. The infant girl's genital sensations correspondingly prepare the desire to receive her father's penis into her vagina. [1945, p. 409]

As a consequence of progressive integration of itself and its world, the child, as we have seen, begins to fear the loss of his loved objects as a consequence of his hatred and aggression toward them. This produces the guilt, sadness, and remorse that constitute the anxiety of the depressive position. In the attempt to resolve this anxiety, the child develops reparative urges and fantasies.

Genitality receives a particular impetus from depressive anxieties and the resultant urge for reparation, because genitality proper is inherently related to reparation, creativity, and concern for the object. In distinction from the activities of other erogenous zones, genitality is not aimed primarily at the relief of tension. It is connected to the urge to create a baby (recall Hans's pleasure at showing how he could dig and "widdle" in the radish garden) and to love and concern for one's mate and one's children (even if only in fantasy). It is a desire to care *for* one's objects, and not simply a desire to have oneself cared for *by* them.

Under the dominance of reparative fantasies and urges, the boy wishes to use his penis, identified with the "good" father he has taken inside himself, as a means of undoing the damage he feels his hatred has done to his mother's insides. Similarly, the girl wishes to have babies as a means of replacing the babies, equated with good things inside the breast and mother's body, that she feels her hatred has damaged.

The classical oedipal wish to have intercourse with one's parent represents the confluence of a number of early fantasies and processes, including splitting of the breast into good and bad part-objects, turning away from the breast to the father's penis as an oral object, which is then similarly split, an identification by means of introjective fantasies with the good and bad part-object parents, the awareness of damage done to the "good" parent by one's aggression in fantasy, the desire to make reparation, and the use of the genitals in an attempt to make things good again. The oedipal wish for sexual intercourse appears deceptively simple. In reality it is a complex structure whose composition (and meaning) is manifold and variable.

Oedipal Development of the Boy

Until the advent of genital impulses, the oedipal development of boys and girls is essentially bisexual. Now, the differences in anatomy and in the sensations arising from the male and female genitals give rise to differing fantasies in the boy and the girl. Oedipal development starts to diverge along two separate pathways, which we shall now trace individually.

As we have seen, in the earliest stages of the boy's Oedipus complex, he turns some of his love and sexual desire from his mother's breast toward his father's penis. In his fantasy, the penis is heir to the breast, and is felt to be able to gratify his sexual desires, as the breast had gratified his hunger, and to fill him with children as the breast had filled him with milk. His attitude toward his father's penis is initially receptive — in Klein's terminology, the boy is in a "feminine" position. This positive, passive-homosexual relationship to the father's penis is the boy's first oedipal position. Little Hans's pleasurable fantasy that a plumber-father would enter his stomach with his borer was a vestige of this relationship, as was his insistence that he would be the next in the family to have a baby, by making "lumf."

This feminine position, with its reassuring picture of the penis as "a good and creative organ," is a precondition for the boy's developing a healthy heterosexual oedipal relationship with his mother, for "only if the boy has a strong enough belief in the 'goodness' of the male genital—his father's as well as his own—can he allow himself to experience his genital desires toward his mother" without paralyzing guilt over the possibility of damaging her (Klein 1945, p. 411).

A predominantly positive relationship to the father's penis gives rise in the boy to a positively tinged identification with it, which enables him to move on to a heterosexual oedipal relationship with his mother. The boy's ability to experience his genital desires toward his mother lays the unconscious foundation for sexual potency with other women later in life.

This positive relationship to the father's penis also helps to mitigate his fear that his father will castrate him, which enables him to better face his heterosexual oedipal hatred and rivalry toward the father. This forms the unconscious basis of his later aggressive potency with men.

On the other hand, the obverse of the boy's early loving impulses, his early sadism, lays the groundwork for the obverse of his healthy sexual and aggressive potency, his castration fears. The boy transfers to the father's penis not only his love for his mother's breast, but his oral-sadistic impulses as well. To these are added his oedipal hatred and rivalry toward his father. Together, they find expression in the boy's desire to bite off his father's penis. This arouses the fear that his own genital will be bitten off by his father in retaliation. (Hans's fear that he was bitten by a horse would be a thinly disguised version of this vivid fantasy.) These fantasies arise out of the boy's own desires and are to some extent unrelated to his actual father's behavior. If a castrating father does not exist, the boy's unconscious fantasy will invent him.

Moreover, a predominantly hostile relationship to his father's penis will lead the boy to identify with a bad and destructive penis, so that his own will seem to him to be an instrument of harm and destruction. It cannot therefore be used as an organ of reparation to resolve depressive anxieties about the mother. On the contrary, the boy will feel that intercourse with his mother is dangerous for her: His penis has become a *source* of depressive anxiety.

Both the fear of a father who is damaged, evil, and retaliating, and the fear that his own penis will damage the mother, tend to undermine the boy's later aggressive potency with other men and sexual potency with other women.

Even if the boy has established a predominantly positive relationship to his father, he may still be dominated by hostile and sadistic fantasies toward his mother. This causes him to feel that his hostility has caused her inside to become injured and poisoned. The boy may then fear his mother's body as a gruesome and dangerous place, threatening his penis in intercourse with her. This is another factor contributing to the boy's difficulties in establishing an oedipal position of heterosexual potency.

The boy's eventual sexual potency depends, then, on his having been able to establish a predominantly positive relationship simultaneously with *both* of his parents. This cannot result from a split in his attitude toward them, since a split would necessarily create either a dangerous (castrating) father or a dangerous (poisonous) mother, either one of which would inhibit his ability to achieve the full heterosexual oedipal position. The required simultaneous positive relationship to both parents can result only from a successful integration of his good and bad objects, mother and father. This implies integration of his love and hatred for them, with the mitigation of hatred by love, to produce good-enough whole objects. This is, of course, no more than the working through of the depressive position with regard to the parents.

Oedipal Development of the Girl

Female oedipal development diverges from the male's under the impact of the girl's earliest genital sensations. As part of her early positive oral relationship with her mother, she conceives of the mother's breast, and later of her whole body, as full of riches. Her positive oral relationship to the father's penis lends her to feel it likewise is a good feeding organ, and together these give rise to a fantasy — an early theory of how babies are made — that the father's penis feeds the mother, filling her with riches and babies. In her identification with her mother, the girl feels that her own "body contains potential children whom she feels to be her most precious possession. The penis of her father as the giver of children, and equated with children, becomes the object of great desire and admiration for the little girl" (Klein 1945, p. 413).

The girl's early oedipal development corresponds quite closely to the boy's early "feminine" position. She does not, however, depart from this position, but retains it as part of her definitive sexual development. Since the girl's good relationship to the penis, seen at first as a feeding organ, is a transference from the earlier good relationship to the feeding breast, the stability of the former depends to a large extent on the stability of the latter. As is the case with the boy, the basis of the girl's positive heterosexual relationships is a positive one with the parent of her same sex. Her positive oedipal development is therefore a mirror image of the boy's.

Just as the boy's hostility toward his father's penis leads him to fantasize castrating his father, which contributes to his fear of a retaliatory, castrating father, the girl's oedipal rivalry expresses itself essentially in the impulse to rob her mother of the father's penis and her babies. This produces a paranoid fear of having her body attacked and her inner good objects (her own "babies") injured or taken away by a bad, retaliating mother. This fear plays a prominent part in the girl's relationship to her mother. Klein regarded this anxiety, which corresponds closely to the boy's castration anxiety, to be "the leading anxiety situation in the girl."

Klein differs on this point with Freud, who believed that women's most severe anxiety was the fear of loss of the love of an external object. This was in line with his idea that girls do not incorporate their parents into a superego and, lacking solid internal objects, are forced to rely heavily on external ones. He cited in support of this the observation that women appear to rely more heavily than men on the esteem of others to bolster their self-esteem.

Klein explained this observation on another basis: Whereas boys are able to reassure themselves that they have not been castrated by seeing that they do in fact have a penis, the girl is unable to detect any evidence that the inside of her body has not been attacked and injured, until she actually bears a healthy baby. The girl's dependence on the love of "good" external objects is greater than the boy's because (by virtue of the constant interaction between internal and external objects) it provides the needed additional reassurance that her "good" internal objects are intact.

The Kleinian Revision of the Oedipus Complex

Although the findings of early analysis confirmed many aspects of Freud's conception of the Oedipus complex, a number of elements of the Freudian picture are contradicted by the Kleinian one. Her study of children indicated that, rather than succeeding one another in an orderly sequence, as Freud had suggested in his *Three Essays on the Theory of Sexuality*, psychosexual stages overlap from the earliest months onward. Genital sensations occur in infancy and interact closely and with great complexity with coexisting oral, anal, and urethral impulses and fantasies, both loving and hostile. In addition, she held (as to some extent did Freud) that the early stages of the Oedipus complex differ from the later ones in containing not only heterosexual components but homosexual ones as well, each depending on the other. This early homosexual orientation is not defensive, but forms a necessary part of the infant's forward thrust toward heterosexuality.

In terms of specific male oedipal development, Klein pointed out that, in addition to castration fear, male oedipal anxiety is related to a number of *internal* dangers, including threats of being attacked from within the father's bad internalized penis and by one's own dangerous impulses, which are both felt to damage one internally and to damage the mother externally during sexual intercourse. The anxieties are especially prominent early on, and were not apparent to Freud because they tend either to be resolved or to become subsumed by castration anxiety during the first few years of life. As a result, the closer development approaches to genital primacy, the more [classical] castration fear comes to the fore. While I thus fully agree with Freud that *castration fear is the leading anxiety situation in the male,* I cannot agree with his description of it as the *single factor* which determines the repression of the Oedipus complex. Early anxieties from various sources contribute all along to the central part which castration fear comes to play in the climax of the Oedipus situation. [1945, p. 417]

She also emphasizes that, alongside the persecutory fears emphasized by Freud (primarily in the form of castration anxiety), depressive anxiety also plays a crucial role in shaping the boy's Oedipus complex:

In his good aspects the father is an indispensable source of strength, a friend and an ideal, to whom the boy looks for protection and guidance and whom he therefore feels impelled to preserve. . . . [For this reason] the boy experiences grief and sorrow in relation to his father as a loved object, because of his impulses to castrate and murder him. . . . Again and again in the analyses of boys and men I have found that feelings of guilt in relation to the loved father were an integral element of the Oedipus complex and vitally influenced its outcome. . . .

Freud in some of his writings (among his case histories particularly in the "Analysis of a Phobia in a Five-Year-Old Boy," 1909)has taken account of the part which love for the father plays in the boy's Oedipus conflict. He has, however, not given enough weight to the crucial role of these feelings of love, both in the development of the Oedipus complex and in its passing. In my experience the Oedipus situation loses its power not only because the boy is afraid of the destruction of his genital by a revengeful father [that is, because of persecutory anxiety], but also because he is driven by feelings of love and guilt [that is, because of depressive anxiety] to preserve his father as an internal and external figure. [1945, pp. 417–418]

In terms of female oedipal development, Klein agrees with Freud that the girl's awareness of not having a penis gives rise to penis envy, which plays an essential part in her development. But she adds that the girl's envy of the penis is not simply due to a narcissistic wound. It is very much reinforced by the frustration of her desire to have a sexual relationship with her father: Klein found in her analyses of girls and women, that the little girl's feminine desire to internalize the penis and to receive a child from her father invariably preceded the wish to possess a penis of her own.

In addition, she differs with Freud about the part that resentment plays in the girl's turning away from her mother toward her father. In Klein's view, the girl maintains an intense attachment to her mother throughout her oedipal development, which is interwoven with her attachment of her father. The girl does not, as Freud suggested, destroy her attachment to her mother in favor of one to her father. Rather, she preserves it, so that it exerts a far-reaching and lasting influence upon every facet of her relation to her father.

Most significantly, Klein's model suggests a radical revision of the relationships between the Oedipus complex, the superego, and guilt:

> The super-ego in both sexes comes into being during the oral phase. Under the sway of phantasy life and of conflicting emotions, the child at every stage of libidinal organization introjects his objects—primarily his parents—and builds up the super-ego from these elements. . . .
>
> The earliest feelings of guilt in both sexes derive from the oral-sadistic desires to devour the mother, and primarily her breasts. It is therefore in infancy that feelings of guilt arise. Guilt does not emerge when the Oedipus complex comes to an end, but is rather one of the factors which from the beginning mould its course and affect its outcome. [1945, p. 417]

This implies, again in contrast to Freud's view, that superego development occurs in more or less the same way in both sexes, and that the female superego is as solid as the male.

In Klein's view, the wish for a sexual relationship with a parent is never fully abandoned, but remains active in the unconscious, finally reaching expression in later sexual relationships. This expression of a long-deferred, deeply felt wish accounts in part for the depth and richness of adult sexual relationships. The resolution of the Oedipus complex occurs not by children abandoning sexual aims toward the parents, but by children, despite their own sexual wishes, allowing in their unconscious mind the parents the exclusive prerogative of a good sexual relationship with each other. As a result, children then take into themselves as a superego a set of parents who do not interfere with children's own sexual prerogatives—an important basis of healthy adult sexuality.

The resolution of the Oedipus complex depends on the child's love being able to overcome (or mitigate) hatred for the oedipal rival. This is equivalent to being able to let the parent who is loved and the one who is hated (the rival) come together with one another. This task echoes the earlier one of allowing the good and bad aspects of the object to come together to form a whole object, and in fact depends for its success on the precedent of the earlier one, the depressive integration of a single object.

The overall relationship between Klein's model of oedipal development and Freud's is contained in the fact that, despite her differences with Freud, her work not only shows that Freud was correct in identifying the Oedipus conflict as the "infantile neurosis" that, if unresolved, forms the nucleus of psychological disturbances in adulthood, but also shows *why* he was correct in doing so: The Oedipus complex is a watershed for all the anxieties, impulses, and defenses of the paranoid-schizoid and depressive positions. Its resolution corresponds to the resolution of these underlying anxieties, a process that Klein had already identified as the vehicle of psychological development.

18

Envy and Gratitude, Splitting and Integration

In her last major contribution to the study of early psychological development, Klein (1957) examined the unconscious operation of envy and gratitude. Although these two attitudes are familiar to us in our conscious adult lives, analysis had shown that their activity in infancy and in the unconscious had profound and unsuspected effects. Gratitude appeared to be an essential part of the loving reaction to gratifying experiences that brings about the psychological birth of the good object, while unconscious envy tended to counteract the love born of gratitude by inhibiting the emergence of a good object. Their interplay is vitally connected to splitting and integration, and therefore to the foundations of psychological development.

Klein supports her contention that envy is opposed to love and gratitude by citing a number of authorities—venerable, if not psychoanalytic—beginning with Chaucer, who wrote in "The Parson's Tale" that "it is certain that envy is the worst sin there is; for all other sins are sins against one virtue, whereas envy is against all virtue and against all goodness." Chaucer, drawing particular attention to envy's quality of undermining and spoiling of precisely what is felt to be good, describes an envious person as one who is unhappy when he sees other men's goodness or prosperity, and who rejoices in their harm. In a similar vein, Spenser, in *The Faerie Queene*, says that envy "hated all good workes and vertuous deeds." Saint Augustine believed envy to be opposed to the creative force of life, and Saint Paul also emphasized the opposition between creative forces and envy when he wrote in his first letter to the Corinthians that "love envieth not." In psychoanalytic terms, envy is felt to damage or destroy the good object and, at the same time, the parts of the ego that are linked to (love) the good object.[1]

Klein carefully distinguishes envy from jealousy, with which it is sometimes confused. The hatred implicit in jealousy arises from the loss of a loved object to a third party. The lost object itself is loved and felt to be good, and it is the object's loss, not its goodness, that is hated. The hatred contained in envy is directed against the very goodness of what is felt to be good. Although distinct, the two are often found together: Jealousy is sharpened by envy of the grass-is-always-greener type, which makes the pleasures others obtain from the loved object seem greater than those one obtains oneself. The analysis of extreme cases of jealousy often shows that this type of unconscious envy has contributed substantially to its growth.

Envy is also found to inflame greed. For example, the insatiability of greed is partly due to envy of what is desired, which, by spoiling its goodness, renders it unsatisfying. A greedy desire to have more than one is entitled to may also be connected to a sense of unfairness at one's not being able to possess *all* of what is felt to be good, which is another expression of envy.

---

[1]Klein was, of course, examining *unconscious* envy and gratitude. There is a form of envy, usually quite conscious, that amounts to little more than an expression of admiration. We tend to recognize it in ourselves with a rueful smile, which itself indicates that it has been greatly mitigated by love. The destructive envy that Klein and her literary forebears were concerned with is deeply unconscious (deeply feared) and quite split off from the feelings of love that might ameliorate it.

Klein points out that in the transference, "the envious patient grudges the analyst the success of his work," because the analyst's success, even when it redounds to the patient's benefit, is an object of envy. Such a grudging attitude may cause the patient to hate precisely what he feels is good about the analyst's work—its love, solace, and understanding—and lead him to spoil it in his mind.

The effect of unconscious envy is illustrated by the following dream of a patient in analysis:

> The patient is watching a man on stage throwing packets of food to the audience. The packets contain something like ham or cheese, and the audience is receiving them enthusiastically. The patient decides that he would like to do the same and obtains some packets of food. But when he throws them to the audience, he discovers that they contain lead weights and fishhooks. The weights injure people by striking them on the head, and the fishhooks cut their hands when they try to grab his packets.

He associated the man on stage with his analyst, and also with an actor who plays faded homosexuals. He then associated him to a transsexual performer, and to another actor whom the patient considered admirable but crazy.

The patient's perceptions of the analyst-performer feeding his audience good interpretation was a positive one (he would like to do the same as the analyst), but it is also tinged with envy (the admired analyst is associated to a faded homosexual, a transsexual, and to a man who is nice but crazy). The envy drives the patient to project undesirable qualities into the analyst, which alters the patient's unconscious perception of him, so that unconsciously he sees him as a blend of someone admirable and someone crazy. When he tries to imitate him, he finds himself crazily throwing out bad and dangerous things despite his intentions. One of the patient's symptoms is that, when speaking in public, he often finds himself saying the opposite of what he intended.

When the patient "feels that the analyst and the help he is giving have become spoilt and devalued by his envious criticism, he cannot introject him sufficiently as a good object nor accept his interpretations with real conviction and assimilate them" (Klein 1957). The analysis thereby loses meaning for the patient. This discovery has great clinical importance: In many instances of analysis having only a superficial impact on the patient, even after many years, unconscious envy has been found at the root of the problem.

Gratitude implies some awareness of the value of what has been received. It forms an important part of the infant's capacity to love its good objects. This must be distinguished from its capacity to need or use an object for purposes of gratification, which does not imply concern for the object, an attitude sometimes ironically called "cupboard love." True gratitude and love for the good object enables the ego to assimilate a good object as such, and thereby to grow by virtue of its contact with the outside world.

The conviction about an interpretation that is necessary for it to have a real impact implies not only a relative absence of unconscious envy of the interpretation, but also gratitude for a gift received. Gratitude is a sign that appreciation for what has been received has overcome envy of it, or, love of a good object has overcome hatred of its goodness.

Gratitude also tends to mitigate the effects of past envy, and to make possible the reclamation of the good object felt to have been damaged by envy, and the revival of one's capacity to love it. Gratitude fosters concern for the good object, concern especially for its fate in one's own hands, which is an essential part of one's ability to see one's objects as whole persons. In other words, it promotes integration of one's objects and one's ego. Klein considered the capacity for unconscious gratitude, along with the tendency to envy the good object, to be to some extent innate. The two appear to be the most direct observable expressions of the infant's primitive loving and destructive impulses.

Of course, external events play some role in determining the strength both of unconscious envy and of unconscious gratitude: Frustration obviously increases envy, and gratification ordinarily promotes gratitude. But we also know that envy may increase in response to gratification (the negative therapeutic reaction, for example), and that gratitude may weather considerable amounts of frustration. We are once again faced with the familiar picture of psychological reality as an alloy of external and internal factors.

Unconscious Envy and Splitting

A successful working-through of the anxieties of the paranoid-schizoid position hinges on the infant's having a "good enough" good internal object during the earliest period of its life, when splitting processes predominate. For such an object to form in the infant's mind, it must split its experiences sufficiently into good and bad so that the good object can be distinguished from the bad. Although splitting is therefore necessary to produce a good object, its function miscarries if it is too wide. Overly wide splitting tends not to produce a good and bad object, but a highly idealized and extremely persecuting one. Klein found that

> so deep and sharp a division reveals that destructive impulses, envy, and persecutory anxiety are very strong and that idealization serves mainly as a defence against these emotions. . . . Infants whose capacity to love is strong feel less need for idealization than those in whom destructive impulses and persecutory anxiety are paramount. Excessive idealization denotes that persecution is the main driving force. As I discovered many years ago in my work with young children, idealization is a corollary of persecutory anxiety — a defence against it. . . .
>
> The idealized object is much less integrated in the ego than the good object, since it stems predominantly from persecutory anxiety and much less from the capacity for love. [1957, pp. 192–193]

Among its other functions, idealization serves to make the good object seem invulnerable to attack from envious parts of the personality that hate it precisely for its capacity to gratify, and that are felt to be overwhelmingly powerful. Excessive splitting therefore acts as a defense against excessive unconscious envy.

Splitting will also miscarry in its task of forming a good object if it is too narrow. In many cases, the inability to make a wide enough split may be traced back to a failure to form the "primal split," between the good and bad aspects of the first object in the infant's life, the mother's breast, and between the infant's loving and hating of it.[2] This produces a primal confusion that, persisting in the unconscious, tends to affect all later relationships.

Splitting that is too narrow also serves as a defense against unconscious envy. Confusion about what is good and bad offers the good object some protection from the envy that would be fully directed against a clearly recognized good object. A vague, confused, or gray world, in which the good objects are not felt to be *too* good, offers no clear targets for envy. In this way, confusion and dithering act as defenses against the envious attacks that a clearly recognized good object might incur, and against the resulting guilt and anxiety. One clinical manifestation of such confusion about what is good is lack of convictions in one's beliefs: In the words that Freud applied to a famous obsessional, if a man doubts his own love, he may, or rather *must*, doubt all lesser things.

Klein identified a third abnormality of splitting that might be called perverse splitting. Here, the width of splitting between good and bad is neither too wide nor too narrow, but the polarity of the split is reversed so that what is known unconsciously to be good becomes bad and vice versa. In analysis, this kind of splitting also seems to be connected to primitive envy of the good object. It is often a major obstacle to be overcome in the course of any analysis, since it is revived in the transference. For example, assume that

> the analyst has just given an interpretation which brought the patient relief and produced a change of mood from despair to hope and trust. With some patients, or with the same patient at other times, this helpful interpretation may soon become the object of intense destructive criticism. It is no longer felt to be something good he has received and experienced as an enrichment. His criticism may attach itself to minor points; the interpretation should have been given earlier; it was too long; it has disturbed the patient's associations; or it was too short, and this implies that he has not been sufficiently understood. . . . Needless to say, our patients criticize us for a variety of reasons, sometimes with justification. But a patient's need to devalue the

---

[2]In referring to the "breast," Klein means to include both its physical and psychological functions. It is both a nurturing object and a psychological entity. See pages 133—134 for elaboration on this concept.

analytic work which he has experienced as helpful is . . . connected to envy. [1957, pp. 183–184]

In perverse splitting, the devaluation of helpful or creative objects is accompanied by an idealization of destructive ones. This type of splitting has been shown by Rosenfeld (1964) to enter into unconscious constellations of fantasy associated with drug addiction and by Meltzer (1972) into the psychopathology of sexual perversion.

Finally, there is the highly destructive form of splitting, sometimes called "fragmentation," directed against the integrity of one's objects and of one's own ego. It seems to be a direct expression of primitive envious and sadistic impulses. Its prevalence in infancy and in the unconscious of adults is associated with two factors, each reinforcing the other. The first is the degree of frustration to which one is exposed, and the second is the degree to which destructive or sadistic impulses arise in response to the frustration. In excess, such impulses make the infant feel that the breast has been shattered by its sadistic splitting. As a result, "the infant feels he has taken the nipple and breast in *in bits*. Therefore . . . the frustrating breast— attacked in oral-sadistic phantasies—is felt to be in fragments. . . ." (Klein 1946, p. 5).

During moments of gratification, the breast is taken in under the dominance of loving impulses, at which times it is felt to be complete. But if frustration brings strong sadistic impulses and attacks-in-fantasy on the breast, even this process may be interfered with, for "the infant's feeling of having inside a good and complete breast may . . . be shaken by frustration and anxiety. As a result, the divorce between the good breast and bad breast may be difficult to maintain, and the infant may feel that the good breast too is in pieces" (1946, p. 6).

Since the integrity of the ego is synonymous with the integrity of its internal objects, primarily that of the primal good object, the breast,

the phantasies and feelings about the state of the internal object vitally influence the structure of the ego. The more sadism prevails in the process of incorporating the object, and the more the object is felt to be in pieces, the more the ego is in danger of being split in relation to the internalized object fragments. [1946, p. 6]

After a certain point, this process begins to feed on itself, so that frustration leads to fragmentation even of the intrapsychic products of gratifying experiences, which then increases frustration. A vicious cycle is then created that may lead to the kind of disintegration of the ego that assumes great significance in schizophrenic states, as Rosenfeld (1952, 1963) and Bion (1956) have shown.

In the schizophrenic states, envy finds its most violent clinical expression. It represents both an attack on the envied good object and a means of making it unenviable. But the same attack also disintegrates the part of the ego that is capable of forming a relationship to the object. It is for this reason that the analysis of schizophrenia consists primarily not of the investigation of the relationship of the ego to internal and external objects, as would be the case in the analysis of a neurotic patient, but of the reconstruction of the pieces of the ego and the object so that a relationship between them may even become possible.

Unconscious Gratitude and Integration

In even the most disturbed personality, normal splitting occurs alongside the various abnormal forms described above. The pathway that development follows in infancy depends on the balance between normal and abnormal splitting, and on the type of abnormal splitting processes present. In normal splitting, the good object is clearly and accurately discriminated from the bad, without being excessively idealized: Klein considered this to be the "precondition for the young infant's relative stability" in the paranoid-schizoid position. The product of such a split is a good object that is felt to contain what would be described in adult terms as goodness, strength, and beauty.

This primal division only succeeds if there is an adequate capacity for love and a relatively strong ego. My hypothesis is, therefore, that the capacity for love gives impetus both to

integrating tendencies and to a successful primal splitting between the loved and hated object. This sounds paradoxical. But
since, as I said, integration is based on a strongly rooted good
object that forms the core of the ego, a certain amount of
splitting is necessary [initially] for its integration; for it preserves
the good object and later on enables the ego to synthesize the two
aspects of it. [1957, pp. 191–192]

Klein's delineation of unconscious gratitude and envy adds
clinical substance to the theoretical skeleton of the life and death
instincts. Gratitude is a basis of one's emotional awareness of the
vitality, creativity, love, solace, and understanding that inhere in
one's good objects, an awareness that raises them above the level of
the psychologically inanimate. Gratitude also implies the love and
admiration of these life-sustaining qualities that compels identification with them, which in turn tends to animate one's inner world.

But these loved objects, because they are felt unconsciously to
be the source of psychological life, are therefore also the target of
intense unconscious envy. Envious devaluation makes the good
object less loved, impedes its internalization, and thereby renders
the inner world less animate. If the capacity for gratitude, shaped
both by innate factors and by experience, outweighs the capacity for
envy, which is shaped in the same way, a good-enough internal
object emerges, whose vitality and creativity form the nucleus from
which the infantile ego derives its strength. Thus strengthened, the
infant is better able to face the severe psychological task of recon-
ciling the good and bad aspects of itself (including its envy), and
thereby accomplishing the work of integration on which its psychological growth ultimately depends.

19

Psychoanalytic Knowledge

We may now return to the problem posed in Chapter 1 of how to arrive at a scientific description of the mind without doing violence to its emotional realities. The psychoanalytic response to this problem is shown by the way in which it arrives at descriptions of an individual mind, which might be called "therapeutic knowledge," and in the way in which it arrives at a more general picture of the mind, which might be called "theoretical knowledge."

Therapeutic Knowledge

How is it that the analyst is able to detect the lines of the patient's unconscious, when the patient is (by definition) unaware of them? Freud found the distinguishing characteristic of the unconscious mind to be its tendency to blend instinct-driven fantasies with external realities to produce the alloy of psychic reality. In this view, external events and biological impulses make their impact on the mind only through their participation in this alloy, the final common psychological pathway for both. Klein showed that this dual origin of psychic reality is a result of the prevalence of projective identification in the mental life of infants, and in the deeper layers of the unconscious of adults. In projective identification, an aspect of the self is, in fantasy, injected into an external object, altering it in various ways, subtle or massive. The object, now an alloy of self and external world, is then introjected to form a piece of the inner world — psychic reality.

Projective identification is the way in which the unconscious perceives the external world. By investing the external world with emotions, positive and negative, projective identification animates it for the subject. This endowment enables one to find emotional meaning in the external world, permitting a subjective rather than a mechanical experience of it. In this way, projective identification allows us also to *recognize* emotional qualities in others, including the love, solace, and understanding that Bion, in the passage quoted at the beginning of this book, called the infant's emotional sustenance. Finally, the emotional significance with which projective identification endows or animates the external world allows it, when psychologically digested, to form part of an animate inner world.

The emotional phenomena of the consulting room that brings an analysis to life arise largely from these projections. Without them, an analysis would be not only therapeutically inert but scientifically sterile as well, since emotion, the stuff of mental life, is precisely what a scientific approach to the mind must *not* exclude.

Although the infant's projection of impulses and internal objects into external objects is a fantasy, it is not merely a fantasy. Infants evoke in their objects, in a realistic and also largely unconscious manner, states of mind that correspond to what they have, in fantasy, injected into them. The infant inside the patient — that is, the patient's unconscious — does the same. The analyst acquires transference significance in analysis by agreeing to make himself provisionally suitable as a receptacle for the widest possible range of projections from the patient, like a child's toy that can become whatever the child imagines it to be. When the analyst interprets the transference with which he has been endowed, he uses the emotional experience that the patient has evoked in him as the empirical basis of a description of the patient's unconscious emotional state.

The analyst's detailed interpretation of the emotional valences of the transference allows the patient to assess the piece of his psychic reality that they represent, and so to connect them to other pieces. The forging of these connections produces psychological integration.

Even beyond this, the fact of the interpretation itself brings the analysis to life by demonstrating to the patient that the analyst can think about what he cannot — that is, what is unconscious to him. The experience of an interpretation goes beyond the enlightenment brought about by content of the interpretation. When the patient introjects the experience of the interpretation, he takes inside himself an analyst who can understand something about the patient's unconscious. This adds in a concrete way to his own sense of having an unconscious about which he himself may know. An interpretation contributes not only to the patient's knowledge, but also to his optimism about the possibility of further knowledge, and ultimately of psychological integration.

This model of the transference allows one to understand why it plays such a vital role in the psychological developments associated with analysis. The analytic management of the transference occurs in three stages. First, the patient projects a piece of his psychic reality — an unconscious state of mind — into the analyst. This is done realistically: The patient projects in fantasy some figure from his unconscious into the analyst, but he also goes beyond fantasy by unconsciously causing the analyst to feel like the projected figure from the patient's unconscious. From the emotional impact of the projection, the analyst may begin to decipher who or what he is in the transference, what the patient is doing to him, and why he is doing it.

This deciphering or assimilation of what has been projected into him constitutes the second stage of the analytic management of the transference. Insofar as the analyst, by virtue of his own analysis, is able to bear the state of mind the patient has evoked in him, he can think about it and put it into words for himself.

The third stage of the management of the transference consists of the actual interpretation of it, giving the patient the "food for thought," represented by the content of the interpretation, and also allowing him to introject an object that is capable of thinking about his unconscious. This helps him to think about his own unconscious, and thereby promotes the integration of his conscious and unconscious minds.

Klein considered the transference to be a continuation of the balanced interplay of projection and introjection that operates from the beginning of life, and is responsible for the formation of internal objects and the growth of the ego from birth onward. Analysis contributes to the growth of the ego because the analytic management of the transference is based on the principles by which psychological growth occurs naturally.

Theoretical Knowledge

An interpretation of the transference made to a patient within a psychoanalytic session — the analyst's translation into words of his emotional experiences as an object of the transference, and what this implies about the patient — is in itself a small psychoanalytic model or theory. It may describe only a pattern peculiar to one individual, or it may describe one also found in many other individuals. In the latter case, it is a more general theory. But even if it is a quite general one, such as the theory of the Oedipus complex, it is no more than a description, more or less condensed, of unconscious psychic reality as apprehended through the emotional impact of the transference. Since a psychoanalytic theory is a translation of emotional realities, its claim to scientific validity rests entirely on its being an accurate description of the emotional phenomena of the consulting room. In psychoanalysis, theoretical research into the unconscious and therapeutic investigation of it are one and the same.

Klein's work shows quite clearly that the never-resolved tension in Freud's mind between psychoanalysis and neurophysiology is itself irrelevant to psychoanalysis. She simply assumed that it is sufficient for scientific purposes to regard the unconscious as operating through, and in fact consisting entirely of, the universe

Freud called psychic reality, without reference to material substrates or physiologic processes.

On first glance, this idea might seem to be a radical and unwarranted extension of Freud's discovery that psychic reality is of greater importance than material reality in neurosis. Upon reflection, however, it is no more than stating the obvious—that brain physiology and psychoanalysis are different disciplines, using different methods that yield different data. Physiologists study the physical and chemical functioning of the brain using the instruments of the physical sciences, to detect chemical and physical quantities. Psychoanalysts study states of mind using as an instrument their own states of mind, as they are affected (unconsciously) by the patient, to detect "psychical qualities." To attempt closure between the two is unnecessary, illogical, and confusing.

Despite Freud's lifelong preoccupation with the issue, the scientific validity of psychoanalysis (defined as the investigation of psychic reality) depends not at all on the ease with which its findings can be brought into register with nonpsychoanalytic sciences. Neither the data of the physiologic laboratory nor behavioral observations made outside the psychoanalytic setting address the crux of the matter that psychoanalysis is concerned with. The scientific virtue of psychoanalysis lies in its power to link together, without denaturing them, the emotional realities that the experience of a psychoanalytic session reveals. These emotional realities, omnipresent even when not observed, are the "many new things" that Freud warned his medical colleagues about in his preface to "Dora." They were "new" to medicine because the scientific medical approach had eased them out of the physician's view.

The psychoanalytic investigation of the mind is reminiscent of the search for knowledge described in Plato's myth of the cave, which concludes with the hope that "there may well be an art whose aim would be to effect the conversion of the soul in the readiest way; not to put the power of sight into the soul's eye, which already has it, but to ensure that, instead of looking in the wrong direction, it is turned the way it ought to be."

Klein contributed to psychoanalytic theory a model of early psychological development whose generality permits an important unification of three central concepts of psychoanalysis: the Oedipus complex, the superego, and transference. In her view, the external Oedipus complex is not just a relationship between a child and the external parents, but is even more importantly a playing out in the external world of the child's relationship with internal parents, the parents in psychic reality. There they exist simultaneously as part-objects ideally good and bad, and whole objects damaged and undamaged. The child's relation with them is suffused with love, admiration, awe, hatred, terror, guilt, remorse, and inspiration.

The resolution of the internal Oedipus complex is synonymous with children's resolution of the paranoid-schizoid and depressive anxieties that mark their relationship with their internal objects. It represents successful integration of this complex internal world, ultimately the integration of the child's love and hatred. The resolution of the external Oedipus situation, the establishment of good relationships with both external parents by which children help to produce an integrated family for themselves, is a mirror of this internal integration. The full significance of the external resolution can be apprehended only in terms of children's unconscious fantasies of what kind of parents they contain inside themselves—their superego.

The child's superego is formed, beginning in infancy, by processes that are manifested in living detail in the transference. Perhaps it would be more accurate to say that the superego continues to form in the transference, thanks to the processes of projection and introjection that underlie transference. Analysis of the transference provides an opportunity for parts of the patient's psychic reality to be reworked, so to speak, during their sojourn in the analyst, and to be reintrojected in an altered form. In this way, analysis alters the actual structure of the mind.

The unification of transference, the superego, and the Oedipus complex brought about by Klein's theories may be summarized by saying that the resolution of the Oedipus complex is so crucial in development because it is a resolution of children's relationships with the internal objects that form the contents of their own minds. The most prominent of the internal objects with which the child must learn to live is the superego, an unconscious melding of his or her external parents and impulses toward them, brought about by projective identification. In analysis, these processes of projective identification are once more active in the form of the transference, but this time in a setting in which both analyst and patient are in a position to observe how and why they produce the kind of superego they do.

"In the young infant's mind," Klein wrote, "every external experience is interwoven with his phantasies, and on the other hand every phantasy contains elements of actual experience, and it is only by analyzing the transference situation to its depths that we are able to discover the past in both its realistic and phantastic aspects " (1952a, p. 54). The study of the transference resolves psychic reality into these components. This offers the patient a chance of understanding the contribution of external events (past and present) to his state of mind, on one hand, and his own contribution to it, on the other. Before this, the conflation of the two made possible the correct understanding of neither.

20

Freud and Klein: A Summary

B efore his discovery of psychoanalysis, Freud was a neurophysiologist who viewed the mind as an upward extension of the neuromuscular apparatus. From this perspective, just as muscle twitches are the outward signs of electrical neuromuscular discharges, ideas and emotions were epiphenomenal manifestations of electrical charges in the mental apparatus.

His colleague Breuer had found that if hysterical patients could be induced to trace each of their symptoms back in time to its first occurrence, the symptom would disappear in a rush of emotion. Freud saw the chain of associations leading back to the original appearance of the symptom as the movement of his hypothetical electrical charge back along a network of neurons, and the emotional catharsis that produced the (temporary) relief of symptoms as the sign of a final discharge of electrical energy.

Reasoning backward, he concluded that hysteria itself must be due to the failure of such a discharge to have occurred spontaneously. The laws of thermodynamics (which were devised to explain and improve the operation of steam engines), state that all physical systems have a natural tendency to run down and lose energy, and Freud saw no reason to exclude from their jurisdiction the physical system of which the mind was supposed to be a manifestation. In hysteria, something was apparently interfering with this natural discharge. He surmised that the normal flow of electrical energy was blocked because a part of the apparatus had been damaged and could not conduct impulses, like a burnt-out component in a delicate electronic device. His reconstructions of his patients' forgotten past, created with one eye toward finding a neurophysiologic cause for hysteria, suggested that the damage resulted from a sexual molestation that had overloaded the patient's sexual neural circuitry. This was the trauma, or seduction, theory of hysteria.

But just as this theory seemed to have reached perfection, it was overthrown by Freud's great discovery that unconscious fantasy, if driven by instinctual impulses, could have an effect on the mind indistinguishable from that of a trauma: There was, as Freud put it, "no indication of reality in the unconscious." From the point of view of scientific methodology, this meant that what he had taken to be a history of sexual molestation could also well have been an unconscious fantasy of a molestation that he (as well as the patient's unconscious) was unable to differentiate from a historical event. Freud's scientific integrity demanded that his phenomenologic observations about the mind take precedence over his theoretical assumptions about its nature, and he therefore rejected his physiologic approach as too naive.

Deprived of a matrix of physiologic preconceptions into which he could fit his observations, he focused on the phenomenology of his consulting room, deliberately avoiding premature conclusions about its significance. He began to treat his patients' emotional states not as epiphenomena of underlying physiologic states but as being worthy of serious consideration in their own right. He employed a technique of open attention, modeled on the patient, and open observation that the neurologist Charcot had employed in his attempts to see new patterns in his patients' mysterious movements. But rather than looking at physical signs, he attended to his patients' communications as a means of assessing "psychical qualities" — that is, to their states of mind. From this vantage point he was able to see "many new things" that were not simply pieces of a physiologic puzzle whose overall form he knew beforehand, but a new world, revealed by a new way of seeing.

The most important of these new things was unconscious fantasy, the stumbling block to his seduction theory. His observations indicated that unconscious wishful fantasies had at least as great a role as external events in the formation of neurotic symptoms. His old theory had pictured the mental apparatus as a passive device, actuated almost entirely by the impact of external events. His discovery of the role of unconscious fantasy required a new model that could take its effects into account. His concept of "psychic reality" answered this need. It is an alloy in which external events combine with unconscious wish and desire. Its logic is not that of the causation he was familiar with in the physical sciences, but one of meaning, significance, and unconscious intention.

He saw that under certain conditions unconscious wishful fantasies could act as instigators of neurotic symptoms, and that indeed "as far as the neurosis was concerned, psychic reality was of more importance than material reality." The motive force behind such fantasies were sexual impulses, which existed virtually from the beginning of life. Neurosis arose when sexual urges of various sorts become repressed under the impact of reality (the Oedipus complex). These repressed wishes and fantasies nevertheless had found their voices in the form of the various symptomatic manifestations of neurosis. The greater the repression, the louder the chorus of neurotic symptoms. Neurosis was not, in his new view, a series of abnormal electrical discharges, but a series of emotional events that had meaning. The apparent meaninglessness of neurotic symptoms was due to their being the simultaneous expression of two incompatible forces, that of repression and that of a repressed wish.

As a part of his study of unconscious fantasy, Freud began to investigate dreaming, using his own dreams as specimens. He developed a technique for considering them that consisted of turning the dream over in his mind, "keeping his critical faculty in abeyance," until a pattern emerged. This was the same open-minded stance he had recently adopted from Charcot for listening to his patients' states of mind. The patterns that emerged from this exercise led him to conclude that dreams were meaningful expressions of forbidden wishes, presented in a disguised form in order to evade a censor in the mind. The wishes were traceable to instinctual impulses.

Freud's realization that dreams had a meaning that could be understood in terms of censored wishes led to a direct comparison between neurosis and dreaming. This placed neurosis once again in the context of natural phenomena, but now it was dreaming rather than electrophysiology into which it was set. Paralleling the forbidden wishes, censorship, and disguised expressions of instinctual wishes in dreaming were the unconscious fantasies and impulses, repression, and symptoms of neurosis.

Since neurosis was due not to an electrical malfunction, but to a conflict of emotional forces in a vulnerable person, the physician's task was not to deliver a quantity of undischarged electrical energy by effecting a catharsis, but to bring to light — against the emotional resistance of repression — the hidden meaning of symptoms, as he had brought to light the hidden meaning of dreams. Once these wishes were brought to light, the patient could form a judgment about them rather than ignorantly repressing them and suffering the consequences. The most revolutionary aspect of this was the insight that repression was a matter of emotion, which Freud called the "cornerstone of our understanding of neurosis."[1]

He enjoined all his patients to report as freely as possible their states of mind in the analytic session. They were to refrain from editing, censorship, or premature conclusions about the significance of what emerged. What did emerge was important not only for what it contained, but also for what was missing. True free association is impossible, because emotional resistances of various types always interfere. But these resistances give clues to the nature of repressed

---

[1]The idea that psychological disturbances are due to electrical malfunction in the brain remains alive in psychiatry even though it has faded from psychoanalytic thinking. It is currently represented by the theory that emotional disturbances and anxiety are due to chemical imbalances in the brain. Since the chemicals in question are known to trigger electrical activity in nervous tissue, the new chemical theory is a variation of the old electrical theory.

wishes; one of the most valuable features of free association is its inevitable failure, which acts as a sort of litmus test for resistance.

The new psychoanalytic approach quickly revealed that dreams and neurosis were not the only expressions of psychic reality. The blending of unconscious wish with current external reality also manifested itself in a third phenomenon whose existence was not even suspected when he began his investigations: the transference. In the transference, a wishful fantasy about an external figure is injected into that figure to produce an alteration in the patient's perception of it. Transferences are ubiquitous, if not always detected, in human relationships. Freud treated them in a unique way, by interpretation. A psychoanalyst, he said, should not cultivate the positively tinged transferences nor evade the negatively tinged ones, as a psychotherapist might in order to gain psychological leverage, but should interpret the unconscious significance of both evenly. Transferences are a convincing demonstration of the nature of the unconscious, and interpretation of the transference is a most powerful tool in the work of uncovering the unconscious.

Freud's recognition of transference and his decision to interpret it consistently set into place the final element of the psychoanalytic method. He could now define psychoanalysis not in terms of its theories about the mind, but as a *method* for revealing a certain kind of information about the mind by the interpretation of transference and resistance. From that point on, it was clear that psychoanalysis rested not on its theories, but on its methodology. Whether a particular theory is accepted or not is a matter of complete indifference, providing only that its acceptance or rejection is made on the basis of data obtained by using the psychoanalytic method.

The distance Freud had traveled in the short span of five years or so since his crucial discovery of the role of unconscious fantasy in neurosis, although vast, did not complete his transformation from neurophysiologist into psychoanalyst. His boldness in observing, sifting, and theorizing about the many new things that the psychoanalytic perspective had revealed was tempered by his persistent wish that psychoanalysis would somehow, in the end, be reduced to physiology.

The most striking manifestation of this belief was his theory that sexual impulses were not simply wishes and fantasies, but the mental manifestations of an undetected physical substance called libido. His adherence to this theory, even as he explored the new territory of fantasy and psychic reality, caused him to adopt a kind of bilingual approach to neurosis. He carefully phrased his most important clinical observations in terms that, while referring to psychological events, could also be easily taken as referring to physiological ones. It is as though he were making constant provision for the day when all of psychoanalysis would have to be translated bodily into physiology. Freud the psychoanalyst saw neurotic symptoms as disguised expressions of meaningful unconscious fantasies, tempered and blunted by the force of repression. Freud the physiologist saw the same phenomena as libido having been prevented from discharging along its anatomically normal pathway, which caused it to flow outward along whatever alternative path happened to offer it the least resistance. From the psychological point of view, neurotic symptoms had meaning. From the physiologic point of view, the form that they took was more or less accidental, like the path of a river that cuts its way through whatever type of rock happens to be softer than those immediately surrounding it.

Freud's analysis in 1908 of "Little Hans," a 5-year-old child suffering from anxieties and phobias, demonstrated the power of psychoanalysis as a clinical investigative tool. The case report also heralded in a negative way the momentous development that still lay ahead: Penetrating and graceful as his analysis of Hans was, Freud failed to appreciate Hans's capacity to identify quite vividly, convincingly, and unconsciously with both of the vital figures in his life. Freud also could not see the chilling effect of the libido theory on his attempts to understand the meaning—that is, the psychology—of Hans's anxieties.

His attempts to analyze patients with depression provided him with the opportunity to recognize and redress the first of these two problems. His analysis of the relationship between different parts of the melancholic's mind gave him his first real intimations of the power of identification to form a complex inner world, a kind of society-in-fantasy populated by people with whom a vital relationship had once existed but had since been abandoned. These identifications were not formed by an impartial registering of perceptions, but by a process that colors those perceptions according to the moment-to-moment fantasies, impulses, and emotions experienced toward the object of identification. Unconscious identification, then, was the fourth creature, after neurotic symptoms, dreams, and transference, produced by the blending of powerful unconscious fantasies and impulses with external reality. The discovery of unconscious identification led Freud directly to recognize the superego as the most prominent inhabitant of the inner world. It is formed by unconscious identification with one's parents.

Freud could now address the second major problem revealed by his analysis of Hans. Upon carefully reexamining the boy's symptoms, he saw that even in the case of a phobia — which he considered "the simplest of anxieties" — the libido theory led to contradictions and unforeseen complications. To resolve them, he was forced to turn his theory of anxiety on its head. Up to this point, he believed that repression caused neurotic anxiety by blocking the discharge of libido. This made the libido "ferment." Fermented libido was experienced not as sexual excitation but as anxiety. The clinical data, however, indicated just the reverse. Repression did not cause anxiety; anxiety caused repression. The cause of neurotic anxiety itself now had to be relocated. He found it in the relationship between the patient's ego and a hostile superego; the latter produced anxiety by threatening the ego from within. The symptoms of neurosis were not an aberrant outflow of libido, but merely defenses erected to avoid experiencing this anxiety.

This conclusion represented a major victory for Freud the psychoanalyst over Freud the neurophysiologist, and it was the pinnacle of his development as a psychoanalyst. He now needed to make one final theoretical revision to account for the hostility of the neurotic superego. His clinical studies of patients exhibiting "moral masochism" showed clearly that during the formation of the superego in these patients, the child's perceptions of his or her parents had been colored by hostile and destructive impulses. This meant that, in addition to the already recognized sexual instinct, there was an equal and opposite destructive one that seemed to have the power to overcome the strength of the child's loving attachments to the parents during the period of superego formation. His studies of other neurotic patients showed evidence that the same was true of their superego formation as well, to a greater or lesser degree. The dual instinct theory, as this came to be called, was Freud's last important theoretical contribution.

It is at this point that Melanie Klein's work articulates with Freud's. She was primarily concerned with the problem of anxiety to which Freud had turned his attention in his later years. She was particularly interested in anxiety's role in inhibiting emotional and intellectual development. Her theories of internal objects are elaborations of Freud's discovery that neurosis is rooted in a particular type of relationship with one's internal objects (of which the superego is the most important). Her emphasis on the importance of psychic reality reflects that fact that this takes place in psychic reality.

Propelled by her interest in comprehending the anxieties that interfered with children's development, Klein adapted the psychoanalytic method to the requirements of children. She concluded that once the method was modified to suit their modes of communication, no modification of its principles was necessary, and that the psychoanalysis of children was feasible and beneficial. She encountered strong opposition to these conclusions from a number of analysts, most notably Anna Freud, who felt that the psychoanalysis of children was neither feasible nor even safe to attempt. Klein responded — correctly, as it turned out — that the objections were not based on experience with children, but on pre- and misconceptions about the nature of children and of psychoanalysis.

Armed with a method that enabled her to make direct psychoanalytic contact with the child's unconscious, Klein made a number of fundamental discoveries with a rapidity reminiscent of the period immediately following Freud's first contact with the unconscious of the adult. She found that children and infants have a fantasy that they create a world within themselves by "swallowing" parts of the external world. This internal world is not a neutral image of the external one, but is colored by the infant's projections of loving or hating impulses into it. From the infant's point of view, this causes the external world to become animated and charged with meaning and significance. Freud's concept of the melding of impulse or wish with external reality to produce psychic reality implies that something like this must occur. Klein's concept of the formation of the inner world is a detailed and explicit description of *how* it occurs. The unconscious mind is literally built up by this phenomenon, which operates virtually from birth, and continues on, in the deeper layers of the unconscious, throughout life. Klein called this balanced interaction of projection and introjection, both operating by means of unconscious fantasy, projective identification.

The infant's projection of love and hatred into the external world causes it to appear to be split into two polarized parts, one ideally good and the other ideally bad. This primal split is a consequence of the infant's urgent need to find objects for both loving impulses and destructive impulses, and to keep the two as far apart from each other as possible, in order to preserve good objects (good both because they gratify and because they are loved) from bad ones (bad because they frustrate and because they are hated). Introjection of an external world formed in this way creates a parallel world of good and bad internal objects.

Klein believed that alongside the tendency for the infant's mind to split itself in this way, there is a countervailing force, also present from the beginning of life, and connected to the sexual or life instincts, that tends to bring the disparate pieces of the mind together. The visible manifestation of this psychic integration is psychological growth: The mind grows by linking together the loving and destructive parts of itself that splitting makes recede from one another. She portrays a painful and never entirely successful struggle by parts of the child's personality capable of loving and embracing life to recognize and come to terms with other parts of the personality that are destructive to those aims. This struggle is reawakened sharply in adult life during periods of mourning. Much of the pain of mourning is, in fact, due precisely to the revival of this painful infantile conflict in the unconscious. Her portrayal of psychological growth in these terms is reminiscent of Greek tragedy in its respect for the inevitability of human suffering and limitations, and in its recognition of the common nobility inherent in struggling against ourselves for partial — that is, human — successes.[2] Insofar as integration is achieved, the mind is able to establish contact with

---

[2]See "Some Reflections on the Oresteia" (Klein 1963).

reality, both external and internal, to differentiate between the two, and to replace the quasi-stable equilibrium it had obtained by splitting with a more stable one nourished by love and reparation.

Klein's discovery that projective identification is the dominant type of relationship to one's objects in the early months of life also led her to revise Freud's version of oedipal development in both sexes. While confirming some of the main points of his theories of oedipal development and superego formation, her model gives much more weight to boys' and girls' (projective) identification with their mothers, and establishes a feminine phase early in the development of both sexes.

Finally, Klein conducted a last investigation into the problem of the life and death instincts, in which she gives them solid psychological specificity by tying them to the clinical realities of gratitude and envy.

References

Abraham, K. (1911). Notes on the psychoanalytical investigation and treatment of manic-depressive insanity and allied conditions. In *Selected Papers of Karl Abraham, M.D.,* tr. D. Bryan and A. Strachey, pp. 137–156. New York: Basic Books.

Bion, W. R. (1954). Notes on the theory of schizophrenia. In *Second Thoughts,* pp. 23–25. New York: Jason Aronson, 1967.

_____ (1956). Development of schizophrenic thought. In *Second Thoughts,* pp. 36–42. New York: Jason Aronson, 1967.

_____ (1957). Differentiation of the psychotic from the non-psychotic personalities. In *Second Thoughts,* pp. 43–64. New York: Jason Aronson, 1967.

_____ (1959). Attacks on linking. In *Second Thoughts,* pp. 93–109. New York: Jason Aronson, 1967.

_____ (1962). Learning from experience. In *Seven Servants: Four Works by Wilfred R. Bion.* New York: Jason Aronson, 1977.

_____ (1963). Elements of psychoanalysis. In *Seven Servants: Four Works by Wilfred R. Bion.* New York: Jason Aronson, 1977.

———— (1965). Transformations. In *Seven Servants: Four Works by Wilfred R. Bion.* New York: Jason Aronson, 1977.

———— (1970). Attention and interpretation. In *Seven Servants: Four Works by Wilfred R. Bion.* New York: Jason Aronson, 1977.

Breuer, J., and Freud, S. (1895). Studies on hysteria. *Standard Edition* 2:3–305.

Freud, S. (1893). Charcot. *Standard Edition* 3:11–23.

———— (1894). The neuro-psychoses of defence. *Standard Edition* 3:47–61.

———— (1900) The interpretation of dreams. *Standard Edition* 4/5.

———— (1901). The psychopathology of everyday life. *Standard Edition* 6.

———— (1905a). Fragment of an analysis of a case of hysteria. *Standard Edition* 7:7–122.

———— (1905b). Three essays on the theory of sexuality. *Standard Edition* 7:130–243.

———— (1909). Analysis of a phobia in a five-year-old boy. *Standard Edition* 10:5–149.

———— (1912). The dynamics of transference. *Standard Edition* 12:99–108.

———— (1916). Some character types met with in psycho-analytic work. *Standard Edition* 14:311–333.

———— (1917). Mourning and melancholia. *Standard Edition* 14:143–258.

———— (1920). Beyond the pleasure principle. *Standard Edition* 18:7–64.

———— (1921) Group psychology and the analysis of the ego. *Standard Edition* 18:69–143.

———— (1923). The ego and the id. *Standard Edition* 19:12–66.

———— (1924). The economic problem of masochism. *Standard Edition* 19:159–170.

———— (1925) An autobiographical study. *Standard Edition* 20:7–74.

———— (1926). Inhibitions, symptoms and anxiety. *Standard Edition* 20:87–174.

———— (1930). Civilization and its discontents. *Standard Edition* 21:64–145.

———— (1933). New introductory lectures on psycho-analysis. *Standard Edition* 22:64–145.

———— (1937). Analysis terminable and interminable. *Standard Edition* 23:216–253.

———— (1950). Project for a scientific psychology. *Standard Edition* 1:295–397.

———— (1985). *The Complete Letters of Sigmund Freud to Wilhelm Fliess 1887–1904.* Trans. and ed. J. M. Masson. Cambridge: Harvard University Press.

Isaacs, S. (1952). The nature and function of phantasy. In *Developments in*

Psychoanalysis, M. Klein et al. London: Hogarth Press.

Jaques, E. (1970). *Work, Creativity and Social Justice.* New York: International Universities Press.

Jones, E. (1948). Introduction, Contributions to psychoanalysis 1921–1945 by Melanie Klein. In *Envy and Gratitude and Other Works 1946–1963,* pp. 337–340. New York: Macmillan, 1984.

_____ (1952). Preface, Developments in Psychoanalysis by Melanie Klein et al. In *Envy and Gratitude and Other Works 1946–1963,* p. 341. New York: Macmillan, 1984.

_____ (1953). *The Life and Work of Sigmund Freud,* vol. I. New York: Basic Books.

Klein, M. (1921). The development of a child. In *Love, Guilt and Reparation and Other Works, 1921–1945.* pp. 1–53. New York: Macmillan, 1984.

_____ (1926). The psychological principles of early analysis. In *Love, Guilt and Reparation and Other Works, 1921–1945,* pp. 128–138. New York: Macmillan, 1984.

_____ (1927a). Symposium on child analysis. In *Love, Guilt and Reparation and Other Works, 1921–1945,* pp. 139–169. New York: Macmillan, 1984.

_____ (1927b). Criminal tendencies in normal children. In *Love, Guilt and Reparation and Other Works, 1921–1945,* pp. 170–185. New York: Macmillan, 1984.

_____ (1929). Personification in the play of children. In *Love, Guilt and Reparation and Other Works, 1921–1945,* pp. 199–209. New York: Macmillan, 1984.

_____ (1932). *The Psychoanalysis of Children.* New York: Macmillan, 1984.

_____ (1933). The early development of conscience in the child. In *Love, Guilt and Reparation and Other Works, 1921–1945,* pp. 248–257. New York: Macmillan, 1984.

_____ (1935). A contribution to the psychogenesis of manic-depressive states. In *Love, Guilt and Reparation and Other Works, 1921–1945,* pp. 262–289. New York: Macmillan, 1984.

_____ (1936). Weaning. In *Love, Guilt and Reparation and Other Works, 1921–1945,* pp. 290–305. New York: Macmillan, 1984.

_____ (1937). Love, guilt and reparation. In *Love, Guilt and Reparation and Other Works, 1921–1945,* pp. 306–343. New York: Macmillan, 1984.

_____ (1940). Mourning and its relation to manic-depressive states. In *Love, Guilt and Reparation and Other Works, 1921–1945,* pp. 344–369. New York: Macmillan, 1984.

———— (1945). The Oedipus complex in the light of early anxieties. In *Love, Guilt and Reparation and Other Works, 1921–1945*, pp. 370–419. New York: Macmillan, 1984.

———— (1946). Notes on some schizoid mechanism. In *Envy and Gratitude and Other Works, 1946–1963*, pp. 1–24. New York: Macmillan, 1984.

———— (1952a). The origins of transference. In *Envy and Gratitude and Other Works, 1946–1963*, pp. 48–56. New York: Macmillan, 1984.

———— (1952b). The mutual influences in the development of ego and id. In *Envy and Gratitude and Other Works, 1946–1963*, pp. 57–60. New York: Macmillan, 1984.

———— (1955). The psychoanalytic play technique: Its history and significance. In *Envy and Gratitude and Other Works, 1946–1963*, pp. 122–140. New York: Macmillan, 1984.

———— (1957). Envy and gratitude. In *Envy and Gratitude and Other Works, 1946–1963*, pp. 176–235. New York: Macmillan, 1984.

———— (1958). On the development of mental functioning. In *Envy and Gratitude and Other Works, 1946–1963*, pp. 236–246. New York: Macmillan, 1984.

———— (1959). Our adult world and its roots in infancy. In *Envy and Gratitude and Other Works, 1946–1963*, pp. 247–263. New York: Macmillan, 1984.

———— (1963). Some reflections on the Oresteia. In *Envy and Gratitude and Other Works, 1946–1963*, pp. 275–299. New York: Macmillan, 1984.

Lindner, S. (1879). "Das Saugen an den Fingern, Lippen, etc. bei den Kindern. (Ludeln.) Eine Studie." *Jahrbuch fuer Kinderheilkunde und Physische Erziehung* 14:68–91.

Mayr, E. (1982). *The Growth of Biological Thought. Cambridge: Belknap*.

Meltzer, D. (1967). *The Psycho-Analytical Process.* London: Heinemann.

———— (1972). *Sexual States of Mind.* Perthshire, Scotland: Clunie Press.

———— (1975). *Explorations in Autism.* Perthshire, Scotland: Clunie Press.

Money-Kyrle, R. E. (1960). *Man's Picture of His World.* New York: International Universities Press.

Racker, H. (1968). *Transference and Counter-transference.* London: Hogarth Press.

Rosenfeld, H. (1947). Analysis of a schizophrenic state with depersonalization. In *Psychotic States*, pp. 13–33. New York: International Universities Press, 1966.

———— (1950). Note on the psychopathology of confusional states in chronic schizophrenia. In *Psychotic States*, pp. 52–62. New York: International Universities Press, 1966.

———— (1952a). Notes on the psychoanalysis of the super-ego conflict in an acute schizophrenic patient. In *Psychotic States,* pp. 63–103. New York: International Universities Press, 1966.

_____ (1952b). Transference-phenomena and transference-analysis in an acute catatonic schizophrenic patient. In *Psychotic States,* pp. 104–116. New York: International Universities Press, 1966.

_____ (1954). Considerations regarding the psychoanalytic approach to acute and chronic schizophrenia. In *Psychotic States,* pp. 117–127. New York: International Universities Press, 1966.

_____ (1963). Notes on the psychopathology and psychoanalytic treatment of schizophrenia. In *Psychotic States,* pp. 155–168. New York: International Universities Press, 1966.

_____ (1964). The psychopathology of drug addiction and alcoholism: A critical review of the psychoanalytic literature. In *Psychotic States,* pp. 217–242. New York: International Universities Press, 1966.

Schlossman, F. E. (1926). Frage des Hospitalismus im Säuglingsaustalten. *Zeitschrift für Kinderheilkunde* 42:31–38, 1926.

Segal, H. (1950). Some aspects of the analysis of a schizophrenic. In *The Work of Hanna Segal: A Kleinian Approach to Clinical Practice,* pp. 101–120. New York: Jason Aronson, 1981.

_____ (1952). A psychoanalytical approach to aesthetics. In *The Work of Hanna Segal: A Kleinian Approach to Clinical Practice,* pp. 185–206. New York: Jason Aronson, 1981.

_____ (1956). Depression in the schizophrenic. In *The Work of Hanna Segal: A Kleinian Approach to Clinical Practice,* pp. 121–130. New York: Jason Aronson, 1981.

_____ (1974). Delusion and artistic creativity. In *The Work of Hanna Segal: A Kleinian Approach to Clinical Practice,* pp. 207–216. New York: Jason Aronson, 1981.

_____ (1981). *The Work of Hanna Segal: A Kleinian Approach to Clinical Practice.* New York: Jason Aronson.

Steiner, R. (1985). Some thoughts about tradition and change arising from an examination of the British Psycho-analytical Society's controversial discussions (1943–44). *International Review of Psycho-Analysis* 12:27.

Strachey, J. (1962). The Emergence of Freud's Fundamental Hypothesis. *Standard Edition* 3:62–68.

Thorner, H. (1981). Notes on the desire for knowledge. *International Journal of Psycho-Analysis* 62:73.

Index

Abraham, K., 95, 149
Abreaction, 21, 51
Aggressive drive, 114
Aggressive potency, 210–211
Agitation, 194
Anal impulses, 165, 172, 213
Anal period, 107, 170
Analysis. *See* Psychoanalysis
"Analysis of a Phobia in a
    Five-Year-Old Boy," 81,
    214
Anxiety, 22–23, 81, 92, 100,
    105–108, 110, 151,
    187–188, 195, 208, 212,
    244, 246–247
  oedipal, 179

persecutory, 185, 189, 191,
    199, 205, 223
Anxiety neurosis, 22–24
  prepsychoanalytic theory of,
    90

Beaumont, W., 5
Bernheim, H., 50
Beyond the Pleasure Principle, 78,
    116
Biological impulses, 232
Bion, W. R., 6–12, 164–165,
    181, 226, 232
Bipolar illness, 195
Bisexuality, and oedipal
    development, 209

Breast, 107, 162, 174,
    205–206, 212, 223–225
Breuer, J., 20, 25, 45, 241
British Psycho-Analytical
    Society, 124, 134

Castration, 38, 90, 106–107,
    109–110, 116, 204,
    210–213, 214
Catharsis, 20–21, 29, 51, 241
Cathartic method, 25, 49
Censorship (of dreams), 47–48,
    244
Charcot, J-M., 11, 47, 138,
    242–243
Chaucer, G., 219–220
Chemical theory of anxiety,
    244
Child development, repressive
    environment and, 148–149
Child psychoanalysis. *See*
    Psychoanalysis, of children
Childhood events, 74
Childhood sexual molestation,
    33
Childhood sexual trauma, 24
Childhood sexuality. *See*
    Infantile sexuality
Children, 12–14, 29, 34,
    36–37, 125, 134, 139, 143,
    147–149, 151–155, 166,
    175, 186. *See also* Infant(s);
    Infantile *entries*
    and the external world, 155,
    166
    the inner world of, 165–166,
    169–182
    and play, 125, 134

psychoanalysis of. *See*
    Psychoanalysis
    resolution of Oedipus
    complex in, 215–216
    sexual fantasies of, 29, 34,
    36
    sexual life of, 37
    sexual wishes of, 34, 36
    and the unconscious, 137,
    139, 143, 151, 153, 155
"Child's Resistance to
    Enlightenment, The," 148
Collateral channels, 76
Conscious fantasy, 161
Creativity, 200, 208, 220
Cupboard love, 222

Darwin, C., 47
Day residue, of dreams, 48–49
Depression, 95, 185–186, 188,
    246
    and mourning, 96
Depressive anxiety, 189, 193,
    199, 205, 208, 211, 214,
    236
Depressive illness. *See*
    Melancholia
Depressive integration of a
    single object, 216
Depressive pain, 193–194
Depressive position, 14, 188,
    194, 199, 208, 211, 216
Destructive instinct, 114,
    116–117
"Development of a Child, The,"
    148
Dora, 43, 55–60, 62, 81, 129,
    137, 142, 235

Dreams, 12, 32, 36, 39, 44–49,
    55–57, 63–64, 68–75, 81,
    107, 109, 117–118, 123,
    137, 160, 177–178,
    195–198, 221, 243–245,
    247
  censorship in, 47
  day residue of, 48–49
  ideas and images in, 45
  interpretation of, 46
  irrational character of, 47
  latent content of, 47, 49
  manifest content of, 47, 49
  and neurosis, 48–49
  and repression, 48
  and unconscious fantasies,
    159
"Dreams and Hysteria," 56
Drug addiction, 225
Dynamic unconscious, 51

Ego, 97–100, 108, 110–111,
    116, 127, 135–136,
    163–165, 172, 186–187,
    191–193, 208, 220,
    222–223, 225–227, 247
  ideal, 127
Emotional development, 166
Emotional forces, 51
Emotional realities, 235
Emotions, 12, 44, 75, 126,
    161, 232
Envy, 219–227, 250
Erogenous zones, 37, 208
Erotic impulses, 105. *See also*
    Sexual instinct; Instincts
External events, 33, 36, 49, 74,
    237

External objects, 186, 198,
    212–213
External reality, 33, 123, 193,
    231–232, 247

Faerie Queene, The, 220
Fairly tales, 151, 175
Fantasies, 9–10, 13, 31–34, 36,
    38–39, 44, 47–48, 98, 123,
    212–213, 231–233
  infantile, 151–152, 155
  primitive, 161
  reparative, 200
Fantasy wishes, 33–34, 36, 38
Female oedipal development,
    211–215
Female sexual development,
    model of, 204
Female sexuality, Freud's
    theory of, 14
Feminine position, 210, 212
Fliess, W., 22, 29, 31–32, 34,
    36, 43, 47, 49, 73
"Fragment of an Analysis of a
    Case of Hysteria," 43, 56,
    77, 81
Fragmentation, 225–226
Free association, 64–68, 125,
    137, 139, 244–245
Free-floating attention, 65
Freud, A., 126–127, 134–135,
    138–139, 248
Freud, S., 8–15, 29–39, 48–49,
    55–69, 73–78, 89–105,
    110–111, 116, 125–128,
    159, 162–163, 170, 174,
    189, 204, 241–243,
    247–248

Freud, S. (*continued*)
  and anxiety, psychological
    theory of, 105–110
  and child psychology, 160
  and the destructive instinct,
    114–118
  and the dialectic of external
    and internal reality,
    123–124
  and Dora, 55–63
  and dreams, meaning of,
    44–48
  and free association, 64–68
  and hysteria, 20–26, 29–37,
    43
  and Little Hans, 81 – 92
  and Oedipus complex, 100,
    203–216
  and repression, 49–51
  and seduction theory, 22–29
  and sexuality, theory of, 37
  and superego development,
    oedipal theory of,
    108–110, 169–171
  and the unconscious mind,
    231
Frustration, 222, 225–226

Genital impulses, 37, 208–210
Genital libido, 76, 204
Gratification, 205–206, 222,
  225
  hallucinatory, 159
Greed, 220
Grief, 187–188
Guilt, 195, 199, 214–215

Hans. *See* Little Hans
Helmholtz, H., 19, 44

Heterosexual potency, 211
Heterosexualtiy, 207, 210,
  212–213
Homosexuality, 207, 210, 213
Hospitalism, 6
Hug-Hellmuth, H., 134–136
Hungarian Psychoanalytic
  Society, 148
Hypnosis, 179
Hysteria, 7–9, 11, 20–39, 43,
  45, 48–49, 56, 61, 73, 74,
  77, 160, 172, 241–243
Hysterical fantasies, 31

Id, 187
Idealization, 223, 226
Identification, 91, 95, 97–98,
  100, 109, 118, 123, 164,
  176–177, 186, 246–247
  introjective, 192
  role in mental states, 199
Impulses, 31–32, 34, 44
  oedipal, 38
Incest wishes, 35
Infancy
  envy and gratitude in,
    219–227
  physiologic model of, 160
Infant(s), 189–191, 193
  breast relation of, 205–206
  and early mental processes,
    162–163
  envy and gratitude in,
    219–227
  mental life of, 159–160, 232
  oral tendency in, 207
  and painful stimuli, 162

and psychic type anxiety,
173
and relationship to mother,
153, 162, 186
and splitting, 174–177,
185–186, 189–190,
192–194
as whole objects, 186–187,
189
Infantile aggression, 110, 112
Infantile anxiety, 81–92, 150
Infantile fantasies, 151–152,
155, 159–161
Infantile neurosis, 216
Infantile sexuality, 38, 49, 55,
57, 63, 75–77, 81, 93,
113–114, 203
Inhibitions, Symptoms and Anxiety,
103–104, 107, 179
Innate destructive force, 134,
174
Instinct, 38, 116–117, 123, 160
death, 227, 250
of infants, for their mother,
153
life, 227, 250
theory, dual, 248
Instinctual drives, 51, 98, 104
Instinctual urges, 160–161,
165, 244
Integration, 190–191, 195, 199,
208, 211, 222, 227, 233,
236, 249
Internal objects, 13, 163, 174,
186, 189 – 190, 192, 200,
213, 223, 225, 232, 234,
248
Internal reality, 123

Internalization, 164–165
Interpretation (psychoanalytic),
62, 138
Interpretation of Dreams, The, 36,
45–47
Introjection, 13, 163–166, 172,
174–177, 185, 189, 205,
208, 234, 236, 249
Introjective fantasies, 209
Introjective identification, 192
Isaacs, S., 160

Jaques, E., 200
Jealousy, 220
Jones, E., 35, 124, 126–128

Klein, M., 12–15, 109–110,
123–124, 126–128, 138,
148, 159–160, 176,
193–194, 232, 234,
236–237, 248–250
and child psychoanalysis,
125–126, 134–143,
149–150, 154, 160, 185
and depressive illness,
194–195
and the ego ideal, 127
and envy and gratitude,
219–227
and fantasy, 159–161
and the intellectual
development of children,
155
and the internal world,
151–155
and manic defenses,
194–195, 198
and oedipal development,
205

Klein, M. (*continued*)
  and Oedipus complex,
    203-216
  opposition to, 124, 128-129,
    174
  and projective identification,
    176-182, 249
  and psychoanalytic
    technique, 139-140, 203,
    248
  and psychological
    development, 173,
    185-186, 235-237
  and schizophrenia, 180-182
  and splitting, 174-176,
    223-226
  and superego development,
    170-173
  and transformation of
    superego, 185-200
  and the unconscious as
    psychic reality, 234-235
Krafft-Ebing, R., 25

Latent content, of dreams, 47,
    49, 160
Learning from Experience, 6
Leibnitz, G. W., 9
Libidinal regression, 76
Libido, 76-77, 90, 98, 116,
    179, 204, 246-247
Libido theory of anxiety, 15,
    75-77, 81, 92, 104, 106,
    120, 246-247
Lindner, S., 36*n*, 76
Little Hans, 81-92, 95,
    100-105, 109, 125, 133,
    135, 139, 208-209,
    246-247
Love, 6, 187, 194, 200, 206,
    208, 211, 214, 219-220,
    222-223, 126, 232

Manic defenses, 194-195, 198
Manic-depressive illness, 96,
    124, 195
Manic reparation, 195
Manifest content, of dreams,
    47, 49
Masturbatory fantasies, 31
Material reality, 177
Melancholia, 91, 96-99, 185,
    194
Meltzer, D., 63, 225
Memories, 10, 31-32
Mental apparatus, 24-25, 48,
    75-76, 241, 243
Mental structures. *See* Mind
Metapsychology, 75
Mind, 39, 118, 123, 163, 232
  of children, 125, 165
  as electrical capacitor, 9
  model of, 8-9
  scientific description of, 231
  in sleep, 45
Moral masochism, 114-116,
    170, 173, 247
Mourning, 96, 108, 187, 249
"Mourning and Melancholia,"
    96, 99, 163-164
Mouth, 37, 76

Narcissism, 194, 215
Negative therapeutic reaction,
    115

Neural processes, 31, 45
Neuronal excitation, 23
Neuropathic taint, 34
Neurophysiology, 160, 234
"Neuro-Psychoses of Defense,
    The," 20–21
Neurosis, 9–10, 25, 34, 36, 38,
    48–49, 51, 55, 61, 63–64,
    69, 73–81, 89, 105, 108,
    110–111, 115, 118, 128,
    169, 173, 177, 185, 235,
    243, 245
  and origins in superego, 171
  psychological theory of, 107
Neurotic anxiety, 100–101,
    106–107, 110–111, 123,
    169
Neurotic symptoms, 34–35, 55,
    74, 105–106, 110, 118,
    123, 169, 243–244,
    246–247
Neurotics, 45
Nonanalytic psychotherapies,
    61
"Notes on Some Schizoid
    Mechanisms," 176
"Notes on the Psychoanalytic
    Investigation and
    Treatment of
    Manic-Depressive Insanity
    and Allied Conditions," 95

Object, 97–98, 98n
  bad, 174, 190–191, 207, 249
  good, 174, 190–191,
    193–194, 199, 207, 212,
    220, 222–223, 227, 249
  of sexual drive, 37

Oedipal conflict, 149
Oedipal development. *See*
    Oedipus complex
Oedipal period, 107
Oedipus complex, 14, 37–38,
    100, 113–114, 170, 185,
    203–216, 235–236, 243
  and bisexuality, 209
  in boys, 204, 209, 214
  development of, 250
  Freud's model of, 203–204
  in girls, 204, 209, 211–215
  heterosexual, 207, 210–211
  resolution of, in children,
    100, 215–216, 236
Omnipotence, 194
Oral drive, 37
Oral impulses, 163, 165, 172,
    210, 213
Oral libido, 76, 98
Oral phase, 215
Oral stage, 98

Paranoid anxieties, 161, 176,
    180, 188, 236
Paranoid-schizophrenic
    position, 14, 176,
    188–192, 198–199, 207,
    216, 223, 226
Parents, 108–114, 116,
    141–142, 152, 189, 200,
    207, 209, 211, 216, 236
  loss of their love, 107–108
"Parson's Tale, The," 219
Part objects, 175, 198, 206,
    209, 236
Part-object stage, 207
Penis, 204, 206–213

Penis envy, 204, 214–215

Persecution, 110

Persecutory fears, 214

Personality structure, model of, 170

Perverse splitting, 224–225

Phobias, 85–86, 90, 104, 106, 110, 246–247

Physiology, 19–20

Plato, 235

Play
  spontaneous, 125, 134, 137, 139–140, 150
  techniques of, 124–125, 127, 138

Primal split, 223, 226–227, 249

Primary process, 159–160

"Project for a Scientific Psychology," 19–20, 44, 77

Projection, 13, 141, 163–166, 172, 174, 177, 185–186, 192–194, 198, 205, 232, 234, 238

Projective identification, 176–182, 190–192, 232, 236–237, 249–250

Psychic pain, 193

Psychic reality, 10–14, 33, 38–39, 48, 74–75, 77–78, 82, 113, 116, 123, 126, 128, 130, 154–157, 177–178, 187, 190–191, 193, 231–233, 235–237, 245, 248

Psychoanalysis, 11–12, 15, 39, 43, 51, 53, 60–65, 68–69, 73–74, 116–117, 124, 126, 128–129, 142, 149, 174,

181–182, 195–199, 203, 222, 224, 231–236, 241–242, 245, 247
  of children, 12, 15, 124–126, 133, 134–143, 149–150, 153–154, 166, 177, 185
  and depression, treatment of, 95
  interpretation of, 138, 233
  and manic-depressive psychosis, 96
  models of, 12, 74
  of neurotic patients, 226
  process of, 50
  of schizophrenics, 226
  theories of sexuality in, 76

Psychoanalytic Treatment of Children, 134–135

Psychological development, 166, 173, 185, 199, 216

Psychological integration, 190–191

"Psychological Principles of Early Analysis, The," 138

"Psychology for Neurologists," 19

Psychosexual stages, 213

Psychosis, 128
  manic-depressive, 96

Psychotherapy. *See* Psychoanalysis

Psychotic states, 180–181

Puberty, 24

Regression, 98, 148

Reparation, 193–194, 199, 208

Reparative urges and fantasies, 200, 206–207

Repressed memories, 25, 29–31
Repression, 31, 38, 48, 50–51,
     55–56, 65, 75, 105–106,
     169, 243–244, 246–247
Resistance, 50, 65, 69, 74, 105,
     138
Reverie, 68
Rosenfeld, H., 225, 226

Sadism, 210–211, 226
Sadistic impulses, 225
St. Martin, A., 5, 6
Schiller, F. von, 46, 47
Schizophrenia, 124, 181–182,
     226
Schlossman, F. E., 6n
Seduction theory of hysteria,
     24, 29–30, 73–74, 242–243
Segal, H., 200
Sexual molestation, 24, 242
Sexual perversion, 225
Sexual trauma, 24–25, 30–31,
     33, 48
  in hysteria, 24
Sexuality, 22–26, 32, 36–38,
     114–116, 210–211, 243,
     246–247
  of children, 37
  development of, 77
Sherrington, C. S., 9
"Some Reflections on the
     Oresteia," 249n
Spenser, E., 220
Splitting, 174–176, 185–186,
     189–190, 192–195, 198,
     205–207, 209, 223–227,
     250

Spontaneous remissions, 182
Strachey, J., 20–21
Studies on Hysteria, 20
Superego, 100, 108–111, 116,
     123, 127, 141, 164, 169,
     174, 180, 185, 189–190,
     204, 207–208, 212, 215,
     236, 247–248
  of children, 127, 141–142
  development of, 169–174,
     185–200
  female, 215
  formation of, 15, 127, 250
  and Oedipus complex,
     170–171
  and origins of neurosis, 171
  transformation of, 185, 190,
     199
Symptomatic forgetting, 65–68

Thermodynamics, 22n, 242
*Three Essays on the Theory of
     Sexuality,* 37, 75, 213
Transference, 56–57, 59–64,
     69, 73–75, 81, 108, 123,
     125, 138, 161, 181, 271,
     274, 232–233, 236–237,
     245, 247
  analyst's role in, 63
  in children, 125, 138,
     140–142, 153
  and Dora, the case of, 81
  dreams and neurosis and, 64
  epistemological role of, 62
  interpretation of, 63, 234
  model of, 233
  as psychological fingerprint,
     60

Transference (*continued*)
 stages in, 233–234
 as unconscious infantile
  impulse, 63

Unconscious, 9–10, 23*n*, 34,
  48, 68–69, 78, 150, 153,
  165, 175, 182, 195,
  232–234, 245, 248–249
 of children, 126, 133, 139,
  143
 and consciousness, 64
 psychoanalytic conception of,
  50
 and repressed emotional
  forces, 50
Unconscious fantasies, 30–31,
  33–34, 39, 48–50, 60, 62,

74–75, 77, 90, 98–99, 123,
  126, 151, 153, 155,
  160–162, 164–165, 171,
  177–178, 181, 191, 205,
  236, 242–245, 247
Urethral impulses, 213

Valéry, P., 49
Vienna Medical Society, 25

Weaning, 107
Whole object, 186–187, 189,
  192, 194, 211, 236
Wishes, 34, 36, 44, 47–48
Wishful fantasies. *See* Fantasy
  wishes
Wittgenstein, L., 5

POINT LOMA NAZARENE COLLEGE
RYAN LIBRARY